Paul Skinner is the founder of the Agenc... that helps clients and partners create Col... organisational success, create economic \...

He is also the founder of Pimp My Cause, which uses cause-related marketing challenges to enhance the capabilities of individuals and teams and supports over two thousand charities and social enterprises with access to pro bono marketing in the process.

In 2014 he was awarded an honorary visiting fellowship at Edge Hill University business school and has twice won Consultant of the Year awards from the Chartered Institute of Marketing.

Additional praise for *Collaborative Advantage*

'Use this book from the pioneer of Collaborative Advantage to grow your business exponentially and make competition for losers'
Sir Tom Shebbeare KCVO
Chairman, Virgin Startup and Virgin Money Giving

'We live in a world where collaboration and collaborative culture are key to unlocking future success. In this work Paul Skinner has set out a highly precious set of gems for anyone tackling a complex task. Whether in business, not-for-profit or social environments, this is a must-read'
Damian Ryan
Author of *Understanding Digital Marketing* and Partner, Moore Stephens

'The new business formula in a world of open innovation and creativity is about getting on and not just getting ahead. Co-operation is no longer a niche. It is a core competence. This book by Paul Skinner, the great advocate of Collaborative Advantage, is a handbook for success in this new commercial world'
Ed Mayo
Secretary General, Co-operatives UK

Collaborative Advantage

**HOW COLLABORATION BEATS COMPETITION
AS A STRATEGY FOR SUCCESS**

PAUL SKINNER

ROBINSON

First published in Great Britain
in 2018 by Robinson

1 3 5 7 9 10 8 6 4 2

A CIP catalogue record for this book
is available from the British Library.

ISBN: 978-1-40871-074-6

Typeset in Sentinel by Hewer
Text UK Ltd, Edinburgh
Printed and bound in Great Britain
by Clays Ltd, St Ives plc

Papers used by Robinson are
from well-managed forests and
other responsible sources.

Robinson
An imprint of
Little, Brown Book Group
Carmelite House
50 Victoria Embankment
London EC4Y 0DZ

An Hachette UK Company
www.hachette.co.uk

www.littlebrown.co.uk

Contents

Part Three: What?
Putting Collaborative Advantage into practice

'In the long history of humankind (and animal-kind, too) those who learned to collaborate and improvise most effectively have prevailed.'

Charles Darwin, *The Origin of Species*, John Murray, 1859

'May this book teach you to be more interested in yourself than in it, then in everything else more than in yourself.'

André Gide, *Les Nourritures Terrestres* (*The Fruits of the Earth*) Gallimard, 1895, translated by Paul Skinner

'Sentiment without action is the ruin of the soul.'

Edward Abbey, *A Voice Crying in the Wilderness*, St Martin's Press, 1990

This book needs you!

I believe you are reading this book at a turning point in history.

I shall argue that creating Competitive Advantage may no longer be in the best interests of your business. Indeed, I would suggest that many of the assumptions embedded in the idea of Competitive Advantage and the models used to create it may actually be holding you back, even when you are not consciously choosing to adopt them. I'll introduce the alternative concept of Collaborative Advantage* and present an approach to creating Collaborative Advantage that can be applied to transform your business, achieve a new level of success and likely change the world for the better in the process.

This book about collaboration is itself the product of collaboration and also an invitation to collaborate. It has emerged from my own

---

* As a word on nomenclature, different commentators also refer to 'sustainable competitive advantage' or 'strategic competitive advantage' among others. These descriptions refer to aligning the resources controlled by an organisation in such a way as to make a superior customer proposition that can confer a business advantage. I use the simple capitalised term 'Competitive Advantage' throughout for simplicity and to make the distinction between Competitive Advantage and the concept of Collaborative Advantage. Similarly, while other authors have used the phrase 'collaborative advantage' to communicate a variety of approaches and benefits in particular contexts, such as following a merger or formal partnership between two organisations, I use the capitalised phrase 'Collaborative Advantage' to refer to the radical alternative way of understanding and developing overall organisational strategy that I have developed independently and on which this book is based.

work running a consultancy called the Agency of the Future and the social enterprise Pimp My Cause. It has been shaped by hundreds of acts of collaboration, many of which feature later in the book. It is an invitation to collaborate in that its value ultimately lies less in what I write than in what you choose to do with it. Reading it should feel like stepping into a workshop to be challenged, to learn from the examples of others, to explore what you might do in their shoes and to work out how the ideas being discussed can help you achieve your own goals. I may serve as a guide but you select the ultimate destination.

Each chapter invites you to reflect on the provocations within it and use the techniques and ideas to build a new strategy for your own organisation, initiative or project. Regular 'quick review' sections will help you to monitor your progress and assimilate the key points into your own strategies for success. Part Two includes a strategic audit that will help you to apply specific techniques to drive the growth of your business by creating Collaborative Advantage.

If my wish and opportunity were one and the same I'd be sitting there with you now, taking you through the ideas and exploring with you how you can use them to help you reach your goals. As it stands this is the closest thing to that I can offer you for the moment – though I hope that beyond this starting point we'll find further ways to collaborate in the future.

The book is structured in three parts to address the questions:

- **Why** should we create Collaborative Advantage?

- **How** can we create Collaborative Advantage?

- **What** can we use Collaborative Advantage to achieve in practice?

Part One proposes Collaborative Advantage as a better goal for business strategy that is more aligned with the needs and opportunities of our times and does more to achieve success in our interconnected world than the conventional concept of Competitive Advantage. Part Two introduces the Outside In framework which can be used to maximise the Collaborative Advantage that you can create by re-imagining the structure and function of your organisation as a platform for collective participation in achieving your goals. Part Three explores the full range of organisational benefits that can be achieved with Collaborative Advantage and illustrates the world of opportunities that can be opened up by applying the concept.

A couple of years ago I read *The English Rebel* by David Horspool and was immediately struck by two things. First of all, by my observation that the period of history covered by the work, subtitled 'One Thousand Years of Trouble-making, from the Normans to the Nineties', means that effectively this history of rebellion is one that extends up to the very years in which Tim Berners-Lee was recruiting supporters to help him build his World Wide Web (which can be viewed as a foundational enabler for unlocking some of the most significant societal transformations of all time). And secondly, by the book's amazing opening line. 'Rebels, unlike rulers, don't often get the chance to build things.'* Indeed, the history of rebellion that Horspool describes is, in the writer's own words, 'a history of failure'. But what will the history of rebellion read like at the end of the twenty-first century? What does a world look like in which rebels *do* get to build things? And what approaches can these rebels use to make sure what they build can last and mark a meaningful improvement on what has gone before it?

The internet and global connectivity may have the potential to radically redistribute power and influence away from 'rulers' – people with money and expertise – and towards people with influence and networks – who may often be 'rebels' in some way or other. At their best, these original thinkers may stand apart for their authenticity

---

* David Horspool, *The English Rebel: One Thousand Years of Trouble-making, from the Normans to the Nineties* (London: Viking, 2009).

and ability to see the world differently. And they may be called upon to enable others to take action according to that worldview. Such 'rebels' see what is missing in the status quo, speak eloquently in favour of new ideas and recruit the support of their peers to build valuable new businesses or create irresistible movements for positive change, capable of delivering real results. In an ever more connected world, with an increasing range of ways to reach out to others in person and online, such rebels do not even have to be extroverts. They may be quiet rebels, able to articulate an alternative vision that can be quickly embraced by like-minded people in their communities and all around the world.

Horspool's history describes the often gruesome fates of a thousand years' worth of rebels. But will the history of the twenty-first century show that the risks today are borne not by the rebels but by the incumbent rulers? What opportunities are there for a rebel to disrupt your industry? And who might that rebel be? Could it be you?

Collaborative Advantage: a better goal for business

CHAPTER ONE

Introducing Collaborative Advantage

The view from outer space

As a tennis fan, one of my most satisfying experiences was watching Andy Murray win his first Slam by defeating Novak Djokovic in the Wimbledon final of 2013, a match which ended a seventy-seven-year dry spell in which there were no male British winners of the tournament. On the face of it, this was competition at its most intense. The world No. 1, versus the world No. 2, in the final of the most prestigious event in the tennis calendar.

And yet, were an alien from outer space to have been watching alongside me, in an attempt to understand how to succeed in life on Earth, what would he have seen? The alien would have seen two men, holding remarkably similar pieces of equipment, hitting a ball between each other within a mutually agreed territory. Our extra-terrestrial visitor would have seen them perform this action according to a mutually accepted set of rules and protocols, both consenting (albeit with varying degrees of enthusiasm) to the oversight of one man in a chair presiding over the game, backed by a group of men and women strategically placed around the court to monitor the placement of the ball within the agreed territory. The alien would have seen the careful orchestration of the boys and girls supplying the two players with the balls they need to play each point and more broadly would have noted the larger context of Centre Court, with fifteen thousand spectators, all turning up at the same time and place, taking their allocated seats through a collectively accepted distribution mechanism. He would have seen the spectators watching closely and maintaining (almost) perfect silence during each short burst of play while making a high level of celebratory noise in between these bursts. And he may well have also been able to interpret the use of the cameras behind and alongside the court and deduced the likely arrangements for millions of people not physically present at the court to enjoy the spectacle. If he'd been given access to a mobile phone and was able to make himself understood he could perhaps have provided a unique commentary on proceedings that could have reached millions of people on social media and no doubt been picked up by the broadcasters and mainstream press!

In service of the creation of one act of intense, career-defining, limit-breaking competition at the centre of the picture, he would also have noted many thousands of acts of cooperation, governing everything from the strings in the players' racquets to the refreshments in the spectators' mouths. So if our guest alien were to write a report to send back home on how humans achieve success, would he not be likely to describe it primarily in terms of how we sew together these countless remarkable acts of cooperation?

Indeed, it is our ability to cooperate in large numbers that separates us from other species.

I remember crouching next to an enclosure at the zoo with my father when I was a small child, gazing at a gorilla that had caught my attention. We assumed the same static pose and appeared equally interested in each other's presence. My father said afterwards that he wasn't sure which surprised him more, the unusually calm concentration of the child or the serenely composed returned attention of the ape. Each might have seemed equally improbable. Yet the reality is that, individually, surprisingly little might separate the ape from the human in the eyes of our guest alien. In fact, even in small groups, our behaviour is not that different to our genetic cousins. But en masse the differences in behaviour are abundantly clear. A Centre Court full of monkeys would be unlikely to comply with the behavioural codes of the All England Tennis Club!

The critical success factor enabling *Homo sapiens* to rise to the top of the food chain was the development of our flexible language, making us capable of expressing imaginative concepts that transcend the immediately tangible world around us to form ideas around which collective organisation at scale becomes possible.* For the alien to report back on his Wimbledon experience without seeking to understand and convey the underlying story that united the thousands of people present in a shared understanding of what they were watching would miss the point as clearly as if the alien did nothing more than report back on the composition of the yellow fluff on the outside of the balls.

Narratives of shared understanding shape our actions and create roles for us to play that in turn reinforce, shape and transmit these stories across whole societies. They are malleable and capable of rapid change to drive new behaviours across communities and populations. With modern communications technology, the flexibility of our imaginative ideas can reach across the boundaries between people, organisations and geographic locations to extend the potential for collaboration exponentially. What could you achieve by better understanding and harnessing the potential that these forces of mass cooperation can bring to bear on the success of your organisation?

---

* Or as Yuval Noah Harari writes, 'The real difference between us and chimpanzees is the mythical glue that binds together large numbers of individuals, families and groups. This glue has made us masters of the creation.' *Sapiens: A Brief History of Humankind* (London: Vintage, 2015), 42.

Creating Collaborative Advantage

Collaborative Advantage is a practical concept that can support you in bringing more of the value-creating potential of the outside world into your business, government programme or social organisation. Whatever you seek to achieve, if you can identify and mobilise the people who have the greatest potential to achieve that goal alongside you then you are on the road to achieving a new level of success.

The book is designed primarily to provide systematic support for people seeking to grow their organisations. If you run a business this approach can help you do more to improve your customers' lives and achieve new levels of goodwill, revenue and profitability; if you run a part of a business it can help you to radically increase the contribution that the activities you lead make to the business and the people it serves; and if you run a charity or social organisation it can put you in a position to greatly increase the positive change that you work to create.

Collaborative Advantage can help you achieve these results by enabling you to:

- Mobilise staff, collaborators, customers, partners and other stake-holders around a common purpose that engages the support of everyone you need.

- Foster improved innovation, better customer or beneficiary experience, increased market reach, greater loyalty, increased income and more ambitious partnerships. A whole host of external contributors will be empowered to become key allies of the business.

- De-couple your potential for growth from the level of resource your organisation controls and remove the upper limit on what you can achieve.

Collaborative Advantage can enable you to achieve more by working with the fuller value-creating potential of the outside world. Creating it, however, is an active process that may require you to understand your organisation in a different way and to discover new approaches to driving its success.

The book presents the Outside In framework that can help you to maximise the Collaborative Advantage that you can create by re-imagining the structure and function of your organisation as a platform for enabling the kind of collaborative value creation that far surpasses anything you could achieve using your own resources alone.

The Outside In framework involves five steps:

- Step One **Find Common Purpose**, the most crucial and the most fundamental step. This consists of identifying what it is that you enable people to do better, framing it in a way that is attractive to them and orientating your whole organisation around enabling this pursuit. This step unlocks powerful calls to action and sows the seed of a new story that will ultimately re-define what your organisation is, why it exists and the contribution it can make to the lives of its customers and other stakeholders.

- Step Two **Create Opportunities** through the design of useful and interesting ways for people to engage in the specific pursuit you have identified in Step One. Whether you supply products, services or other offerings, what matters most is how people use what you deliver and the role it plays in their lives or work. Enhancing this experience is a powerful route to success.

- Step Three **Engage Participation** to create an environment conducive for the kind of pursuit that you have defined in Step One and enabled in Step Two. This is about defining the 'rules of your game', creating different roles – for example, for different stakeholder groups or for people with differing levels of interest and commitment to play – and creating the social customs, habits and rituals that support people in participating in your offerings along-side each other.

- Step Four **Iterate and Accelerate** by developing a deeper under-standing of your early adopters in order to be able to better address their needs and to use their influence to reach a broader mainstream.

- Step Five **Build Partnerships** by identifying partners who can help you to grow faster and further than you could alone. We'll analyse the types of partnership that can create most value for your business and explore how to make them work best.

Collaborative Advantage articulates a way of doing business that can be both more profitable and create greater benefits for customers as well as for the communities they live in. It can be used to bring fulfil-ment to the aspiration expressed by Richard Branson in the Global Transformation Forum in 2017 that a business should be 'an idea to improve people's lives'.

It is not against free markets nor does it deny that customer choice is a powerful driver of the value creation process. On the contrary, my proposed approach not only accepts that observation, but goes much further by showing how even greater value can be created when consumers and the full range of a business's stakeholders not only make their own choices but also have the opportunity to go beyond that to become active participants and contributors to the success of the business.

As the Wimbledon example has shown, I do not argue that competi-tion and collaboration are opposites. Indeed, I readily concede that a great rivalry can be one of life's most thrilling pleasures! However, I hope to develop a strong case to suggest that competition is now no longer the most helpful metaphor we can use to help us design organi-sational strategy and that models of creating Competitive Advantage are becoming increasingly broken. In particular, their core assumption that value should be created exclusively inside the business no longer stands. Indeed, businesses are becoming more and more effective at harnessing the value that can be created outside the organisation by customers, users, supporters and partners.

In this book we'll discover how Collaborative Advantage is better aligned with:

- The demands and opportunities of our increasingly interconnected world.

- A more accurate understanding of the processes of value creation.

- The challenges of an increasingly complex and surprising business landscape.

- A true understanding of human decision-making.

- The explosion in collaborative business models.

....

The Outside In framework is a tool that can be used to systematically maximise the contribution you can bring from the outside world into your business.

....

It can be argued that most business problems and indeed most of society's problems pose challenges that we cannot address alone. Where our success depends on the participation of others we are reliant on tools of influence rather than on tools of control. Collaborative Advantage can help us to forge a path to success that effectively engages people we are not in charge of in helping us achieve our goals. And the Outside In framework is a tool that can be used to systematically maximise the contribution that the outside world can make to a business, charitable organisation or government programme.

What could you achieve with more of the world on your side?

Quick review

- Competition and collaboration are not necessarily opposites – but creating Collaborative Advantage can be a much better way of understanding how your business can achieve the greatest possible success.

- Our human ability to form ideas that enable cooperation may be our most important distinguishing capability as a species. And businesses can represent powerful cooperation-enabling ideas.

- Collaborative Advantage can help you achieve a new level of success by bringing more of the value-creating potential of the outside world inside your business.

- This can involve re-thinking what the business is and what it enables the world to do better.

- The Outside In framework can be used to better engage the outside world by helping you:

  - Find Common Purpose

  - Create Opportunities

  - Engage Participation

  - Iterate and Accelerate

  - Build Partnerships

- Creating Collaborative Advantage is better aligned than models of Competitive Advantage with how value is created in our interconnected world, with how the business fits in with its customers' lives and with how people make choices and decisions in practice.

CHAPTER TWO

The rise of Competitive Advantage

Competition and the birth of strategy

Before we explore the implications and techniques of Collaborative Advantage in greater detail, it is worth situating the concept against the backdrop of its predecessor. Although I argue that Competitive Advantage is no longer the most useful way to develop strategy, it has nevertheless hitherto been one of the most successful ideas in the history of business.

Indeed, the history of business strategy so far can be seen as essentially a story built on four different versions of the same idea: that businesses must compete to win.*

The four versions of the idea were in their own different ways developed by the three pioneers of strategic consulting and the most prominent business school professor of all time, namely, Bruce Henderson (founder of the Boston Consulting Group), Bill Bain Jr (founder of Bain & Company), Fred Gluck (former chief executive officer of McKinsey) and Michael Porter (Bishop

---

* Walter Kiechel III's *The Lords of Strategy*, published in 2010 by the Harvard Business Review Press, has been an invaluable source of information on the history of strategic consulting for this chapter and is well worth a read for anyone interested in the topic.

William Lawrence University Professor at Harvard Business School).

Something that is hard to imagine today is that, before the work of these men began in the early 1960s, the concept of 'business strategy' barely existed as an identifiable idea. At Harvard Business School, the major programme required of all business school students was not strategy, but 'business policy'. Management training appeared to focus more on how to fit in and follow due process rather than how to develop new business advantage. Management practice revolved around 'planning', an often internally focused and highly bureaucratic process. And strategic consulting did not even feature among the list of available services of the world's leading business advisers, McKinsey.

Two factors drove the success of the idea of Competitive Advantage. The first was the ability to package the concept in a marketable form. This heralded what might be called the first 'retail promotion' of a business idea. The second was a backdrop of market de-regulation, with waves of globalisation and the dawn of the internet, all of which served to substantially increase the percentage of human and organisational activity that was subject to competition, as well as the speed, breadth and intensity of that competition. Compared to today's business environment, some areas of corporate life might have appeared somewhat sleepy to today's managers, accustomed as they now may be to reaching under their pillow to check their Twitter feed at 2.00 a.m.

Bruce Henderson, the Boston Consulting Group

In 1964, led by business maverick Bruce Henderson, the Boston Consulting Group (or rather as it was known then, rather incongruously, the Management Consulting Division of Boston Safe Deposit), initiated the marketing of business ideas. They began with the launch of 'Perspectives': short essays to explain to managers and leaders how to unlock fresh business advantage. They also launched the 'invitation-only' business conference format for a select range of business officers – concluding in the early stages, perhaps unsurprisingly, that they as consultants had more to learn than the invited practitioners.

In 1965, as the firm changed its name to the Boston Consulting Group, it decided to focus on 'business strategy', a field that at the time was unoccupied. The positioning on marketing ideas continued with a greater attention to developing new insights from within the firm as opposed to re-packaging existing business wisdom. But the real breakthrough came with the invention of a new tool that would have a profound impact in both raising the awareness of competitive strategy and on changing the way the largest and most powerful corporate organisations conceived of, designed and implemented strategic plans.

In 1966, in response to the problems that a client organisation, General Instruments, was having with matching competitors' prices for television set components, Bruce Henderson and a new consultant at the firm looked at existing research into organisational learning curves. They then took a creative and analytical leap in the creation of a new 'experience curve'. The learning curve posited that the cost of labour in producing an item declines as volume increases due to a learning effect that drives efficiency and Bruce and his young protégé took inventive steps. Firstly, they integrated all costs – not just the cost of labour – and, secondly, they equated volume with market share, in recognition of the fact that the firm with the greatest learning or 'experience' would necessarily have achieved the greatest efficiency and lowest costs. This conclusion provided great reassurance to the market leaders in any given industry and a wake-up call for everyone else. The experience curve demanded that executives consider their positions and formulate their strategy with a primary regard to the position on the curve they occupied in relation to their competitors – and it was this major new external focus that catalysed competition as the new organising principle for business success.

The tool was also used alongside measures of market growth as the basis for the development of the first consulting 'product': the application by the Boston Consulting Group of their subsequent Growth Share Matrix to client organisations. This became one of the most iconic management consulting tools of all time, allowing the firm to plot lines of business at a client organisation in a matrix where they would be categorised as cash cows (high market share, low market growth), stars (high market share, high market growth), dogs (low market share, low market growth) or question marks (low market share, high market growth). The implications for senior management lay in how they should manage their portfolio of business units according to their relative competitive strength, typically harvesting profit from cash cows, investing in stars, disposing of dogs and choosing whether to strongly back or pull away from question marks.

Bill Bain Jr, Bain & Company

The second major embodiment of the concept of competition-based business strategy came in the form of Bill Bain. Bain began his career at the Boston Consulting Group, where he led a division that was set against the two other divisions of the group in an artificially managed internal competition to see which could generate the most profits. Ironically, when Bain's division prevailed, this resulted in the group vice-president and most of his senior players at the division deciding their victory indicated they could go it alone. They left the Boston Consulting Group to found Bain & Company which went on to become one of the Boston Consulting Group's most dangerous rivals.

Bain & Company adopted a similarly relentless focus on competitive strategy and they centre their attention to this day on the three 'C's

– costs, customers and competitors. A key difference, however, came in the way they structured client relationships. They sought to differentiate themselves not by delivering strategic reports or plans as finished products but rather by embedding themselves within a client organisation and delivering a strategic competitive capability through an ongoing relationship that, month-by-month, would support the client's bottom line, then ultimately the value of their shares. This was boiled down into the key proposition not of selling 'advice by the hour' but rather of selling 'profits at a discount'. To reflect the Competitive Advantage they could bestow, unlike the Boston Consulting Group they would only ever work for one client within any particular industry and would carefully track the stock performance of their clients versus those of their competitors. And in contradistinction to the Boston Consulting Group's externally facing thought-leadership strategies, they kept as much of their knowledge secret as possible, rarely divulging their expertise beyond their client base, in a way which served further to arouse intrigue and mystique.

The Bain & Company approach to competitive strategy integrated the positioning-based strategies that the Boston Consulting Group first developed with a more process-oriented approach. They began by seeking to identify and configure client strategy around 'best practices' that reflected the best processes available within the organisation, then evolved to look at 'best competitive practices', reflecting the best practices within a given industry or competitive group and ultimately developed their propositions and advice based on analysing 'best feasible practices' to integrate the best processes available across industry boundaries, highlighting the role of learning across different sectors of the economy.

The formula worked. By the 1980s Bain & Company represented one of the most successful business models in strategic consulting. While a consulting firm could bill its partners out for around fifty per cent of their available time, with much of the remaining time being spent on business development and other supporting activities, Bain & Company were able to bill partners for ninety per cent of their working time due to their long-term client relationships.

And in what may be seen as the apotheosis of the Bain & Company approach, in 1983 they formed a sister organisation called Bain Capital, a private equity firm that would raise funds and invest them speculatively in companies that could be given the full Bain & Company approach to grow their value.

Fred Gluck, McKinsey

The creation of the market for strategy consulting by the Boston Consulting Group and Bain & Company eventually provoked the leading firm of business advisers to develop their own competitive response. The lynchpin of the McKinsey counter-strike came in the shape of Fred Gluck, who at the time of his first salary review was willing to go out on a limb and report that he thought the firm didn't know what they were doing when it came to strategy. The strategic advisory practice at the time at McKinsey revolved around little more than strategic gap analysis, through which McKinsey would draw a client's attention to the gap between their current performance and their goals and objectives and the client would typically respond that the initiatives they were working on would fill the gap. This led to a regular and frustrating stalemate.

Having identified the problem, Gluck was given responsibility for resolving it. The approach he and the firm developed was to focus on a complete approach to strategic management, with an acute awareness of market conditions and competitor performance as well as macro-environmental trends. Strategic management to create the future was heralded as the next phase in the evolution of planning. This went beyond the previous phases of business planning, referred to in chronological order of advancement as financial planning to meet the budget, forecast planning to predict the future and externally oriented planning to think strategically. They developed holistic tools such as the nine-box matrix to support portfolio management and their 7S framework for change management. The real difference McKinsey brought was the capability to encompass the totality of strategic management in their vision and in their ability to execute on behalf of clients. Ultimately, they became the leading firm in strategic consultancy despite coming late to the game. Fred Gluck eventually rose to the position of chief executive officer.

Michael Porter, Harvard Business School

The real king of competitive strategy, the man who did most to create the concept of Competitive Advantage, came from Harvard Business School. He was no less a maverick, having had to overcome serious obstacles to develop his young career. Academics at the business school favoured asking questions about individual cases and avoided generalising theories. The aim was to provoke students into fresh contemplation of each new case study according entirely to its own merits without recourse to broader external frameworks.

Porter, however, arrived at the business school with a PhD in micro-economics, a subject that then revolved around developing models to be used for simulation and prediction at a market-wide level, but not to identify how to make changes to enable individual businesses to succeed. He sought to bridge the divide between economic approaches and those of the business school. Reacting against the two extremes of either ignoring the individual circumstances of a business entirely or focusing on nothing else but these specifics, Porter sought to develop frameworks that could draw on the analytical rigour of an economist but for the purpose of enabling individual managers to focus their thinking and develop their strategy. As he put it retrospectively, in an interview with Walter Kiechel III, 'What I've come to see as probably my greatest gift is the ability to take an extraordinary, complex, integrated, multi-dimensional problem and get my arms around it conceptually in such a way that helps, that informs and empowers practitioners to actually do things."[*]

In so doing he not only matched the Boston Consulting Group's approach to thought leadership and the development of marketable business ideas, he went further, to develop what could be described as a 'unified theory of competition' through his books *Competitive Strategy* and *Competitive Advantage*.[†] Arguably, Porter contributed even more to the development of thinking on competitive strategy than the Boston Consulting Group, Bain & Company and McKinsey combined. He is to this day the business school professor most cited by academics and likely the best known to business practitioners. The best-known components of his approach are the Five Forces (to determine where to compete in the first place) and the Value Chain (for analysing how to create Competitive Advantage).

According to the Five Forces model, the essential key for identifying a favourable market in which to operate is understanding the structural conditions that predominate. The analysis of a market's attractiveness includes a focus on industry competitors, buyers, suppliers, alternative products or substitutes and the potential for new market entrants.

---

* Walter Kiechel III, *The Lords of Strategy: The Secret Intellectual History of the New Corporate World* (Boston: Harvard Business Review Press, 2010), 122.
† Michael E. Porter, *The Competitive Strategy: Techniques for Analysing Industries and Competitors* and *Competitive Advantage: Creating and Sustaining Superior Performance* (New York: Free Press, 1980 and 1985).

The Value Chain views the firm as a system for creating Competitive Advantage in which all its constituent parts need to be aligned around a strategy to create superior profitability through a unique configuration of inputs, processes and outputs. The idea was tied to Porter's claim that organisations must make a clear choice to compete on the basis of lower costs, differentiated product or through a focus on a particular market segment. To be stranded in a no-man's land in between these approaches could be viewed by advocates of Porter's aproach as organisational suicide.

....

Has the story of Competitive Advantage now started to sound false? Could the dominant idea that has guided business strategy for the past fifty years now be on the wane?

....

Competition takes all?

On the shoulders of these giants, competition has remained the dominant metaphor for business and organisational strategy and lived at the heart of the stories we have told ourselves about what being in business is all about. The passing of time has changed its emphasis and highlighted some of its limitations, however. Right from the start, the criticism was that people, community and culture were missing from the analytical tools of competitive strategy. Alternative approaches that focused more on organisational learning certainly rose up the agenda with the coming to prominence of Japanese manufacturing giants. But it has nevertheless appeared so far that none of the alternatives could be embedded in a paradigm as clear, compelling and intuitively right as the concept of creating Competitive Advantage.

Quick review

- Competitive Advantage has contributed greatly to how we understand business and how we create value.

- It is perhaps the most successful idea in the history of business and shapes many of our assumptions both consciously and unconsciously, perhaps influencing our thinking far more than we realise.

- It defined early approaches to how we understand strategy in the particular context of business, as opposed to those of politics or warfare.

- It was pioneered primarily by financiers and focused on controlling resources to achieve superior outcomes to competitors.

- There have been significant criticisms of the concept but previously no alternatives have been developed that have proven as clear and compelling for mainstream use.

CHAPTER THREE

The fall of Competitive Advantage

Has the story of Competitive Advantage now started to sound false? Could the dominant idea that has guided business strategy for the past fifty years now finally be on the wane? The thrill of competition is clearly deeply ingrained in human nature and the idea of competition itself is no doubt as alive and kicking as it ever was. But a number of drivers are making the idea of generating Competitive Advantage less relevant as an *organising principle* of strategy. And I believe that, more broadly, it is becoming less effective in helping us to understand how to achieve the greatest possible success in our contemporary world.

Trying to be the best?

As a metaphor, competition often leads to inappropriate goals and objectives. The idea boils down too quickly to the pursuit of being 'the best', which all too often translates into a race to the bottom and inevitable price wars. Replicating the offering of a rival and simply trying to offer more of the same for less is a key to destroying economic value rather than creating it. This is a weakness in the competition metaphor that Michael Porter, the high priest of competitive strategy, seems to recognise himself. He was asked by Joan Magretta what common strategic mistakes he sees companies make: 'The grand-daddy of all mistakes is competing to be the best, going down the same path as everybody else and thinking that somehow you can achieve better results."

The kind of Competitive Advantage Porter advocated was a competition to be different. That's all well and good, but is that really what we think of when asked to compete? Is there not something in the metaphor itself that is bound to cause the very strategic errors that Porter criticises?

The tyranny of the accountants

A further major weakness in the evolution of competitive strategy may stem from the field having been overly dominated by financiers who are better qualified to support some types of business improvement than others.

We've discussed the key pioneers of Competitive Advantage who came from remarkably similar backgrounds, each studying engineering followed by economics. At the time, their financial acumen and organising power brought new opportunities and insight to the senior management teams of major global corporations that needed to better manage their portfolios of business units and product lines and make better sense of what previously was a murky and muddled field of financial management. For – in many cases – the first time, CEOs were empowered with the knowledge of which of their business units were creating value for the company and which were destroying value or earning less than could be achieved by investing elsewhere. This insight enabled much greater sophistication in portfolio management.

* Joan Magretta, *Understanding Michael Porter: The Essential Guide to Competition and Strategy* (Boston: Harvard Business Review Press, 2012), 187.

Nevertheless, it could be argued that the major thrust of strategic consultancy in practice has been to restrict business thinking to a focus on driving efficiency and cost-cutting, often bringing in new methods and approaches that management teams themselves may have been too squeamish to bring in alone. But business success is as much about creativity and vision as it is about financial management. As one commentator put it using a cricket analogy: 'Financiers can keep tally, but they can't score any runs' or, as another framed it, 'Boards do three things: they make money, they spend money and they count money. But any idiot can do the last two of these things.' Who would you rather have in your upcoming board meeting: a financial analyst or the next Richard Branson?

John Maynard Keynes wrote of a 'principle of no variation'.* Essentially, his argument was that econometric models can only be used to predict future performance where there is no variation among variables located outside the analysis. This was a Keynesian spin on the ubiquitous phrase among economists, *ceteris paribus* – 'all other things being equal'.

The trouble is, as Keynes shrewdly observed himself, that all things are never equal. If economics is the study of supply and demand, it is marketing that develops and defines the form in which supply and demand meet and it is in the chemistry of that junction point that the true ceiling on performance levels is set.

Who are your competitors anyway?

A related point is that industry boundaries are becoming more porous and the provenance of future competitors more disparate and hard to

* John Maynard Keynes, *The General Theory of Employment, Interest and Money* (London: Macmillan, 1936).

predict. Analysing the performance of your close 'strategic group' – the term from competition strategy to describe your most similar rivals in terms of size and offering – can leave you vulnerable to blind-side attacks from outside your sector or cause you to leave your most promising opportunities for innovation on the table. Educational publishers might do better to look at Amazon than at each other; broadcasters might be better off analysing Netflix than other broadcasters and white goods manufacturers might be encouraged to learn more from companies specialising in connected devices than from rival product ranges.

Don't get me wrong; understanding existing market performance, dynamics and conditions is necessary for the development of sound strategy. Necessary, but not sufficient. The most exciting break-through innovation often occurs against existing market trends and is inspired by looking across market boundaries to broader cultural shifts for breakthrough ideas that change the dynamics of an industry. A well-known example is Cirque du Soleil, created at a time when the circus industry was in substantial decline and when industry economic conditions appeared extremely unfavourable for dramatic new growth. But by incorporating ideas and practices from theatre and musicals the founders of Cirque du Soleil were able to re-invent the circus to bring it more into line with current culture. Animal acts were out, original musical scores and compelling storylines were in. The result was a major global blockbuster that has delighted audiences the world over.[*]

* Cirque du Soleil is featured in a prominent case study of innovation across industry boundaries in W. Chan Kim and Renée Mauborgne, *Blue Ocean Strategy* (Harvard Business Review Press, 2005).

Broken models

A further problem that has revealed itself with competitive strategies is that they often fail even on their own terms. This itself is not a new phenomenon. Indeed, a criticism of many of the tools of competitive strategy is that they can often mislead practitioners because they provide a narrative the underpinnings of which do not hold firm for many businesses.

Ever since the creation of the Boston Consulting Group's Growth Share Matrix, a key part of starting a new consulting project has often revolved around 'building the model'. But these models have been based on assumptions that can often prove wrong. In the case of the Boston Consulting Group's first model, it was simply not the case that experience led in practice to the cost reductions predicted by their curve – for example, costs could often be reduced only up to a specific level of volume that justified ownership of particular capital equipment and beyond that scale no further cost advantage was likely to accrue.

The 2008 financial collapse that led to a global economic downturn can in many ways be read as the ultimate failure of econometric models divorced from sound human judgement.

Ever-diminishing returns

A further criticism of Competitive Advantage comes from its own insiders. Consultants have measured the durability of Competitive Advantage and found that since the 1960s the sustainability of Competitive Advantage has been in ever-accelerating decline.* Agility

* See for example the study by Robert R. Wiggins of the University of Memphis and Timothy W. Ruefli of the University of Texas, *Sustained Competitive Advantage: Temporal Dynamics and the Incidence and Persistence of Superior Economic Performance, Organization Science*, Vol. 13, No.1, Jan–Feb 2002.

and responsiveness can count for more than deeply entrenched positions that can leave an organisation more vulnerable than dominant.

Changing business models

More broadly, the concept of Competitive Advantage does not appear to explain the structuring mechanics of the more collaborative business models that have driven so many of the most successful and fast-growing organisations of recent years, including the businesses that form what has come to be called the 'sharing economy'.

For example, where Disney has built its success on the assets that it owns, especially its universally recognised characters, YouTube is dependent on its users for the creation of its core value; where the *Encyclopaedia Britannica* depends on its roster of expert contributors, Wikipedia depends on the open engagement of a worldwide community of volunteers; and where large hotel chains depend on their staff and the property they own and rent, Airbnb depends on the spare rooms and friendly welcome of millions of users opening up their own homes. These organisations pose fundamental challenges to pre-existing concepts of what a book, a room or a film should be, who should provide them and how they should be used.

Shareholder value versus stakeholder value

Outside business, people may be more likely to lead the charge against Competitive Advantage based on its apparent failure to accommodate broader goals than shareholder value. This can lead to what economists call 'negative externalities' – when a business retains its profits for its shareholders but imposes costs on society. These could range from anything like litter or noise pollution to driving climate change and environmental degradation, meaningful costs that an organisation may cause but for which it may not be liable to pay. This can lead to a backlash from communities, the media and politicians and ultimately can put what you might call a business's 'licence to operate' in jeopardy. It can also lead organisations to miss out on the positive advantages that can accrue in creating a more positive total contribution to social or stakeholder value.

Consumers don't care about increasing shareholder value when they make their purchase decisions. They do care about choosing products, services and companies that they believe make a meaningful contribution to improving their lives. When Virgin Trains lost their franchise to run the mainline West Coast Main Line in the UK, a major force for compelling the British government to re-think its position came in the form of the voices of Virgin customers. An e-petition demanding that Virgin continue to run the service was started not by the Virgin Group itself but by Ross McKillop, a regular customer of Virgin Trains and reached one hundred thousand signatures in a week. These included the names of celebrities such as Stephen Fry and Derren Brown. Which business leader would choose to live without that kind of support?

A better understanding of how we make decisions

Finally, the econometric models underpinning competition strategy do not paint a true picture of how people behave in practice. The models on which competitive strategies are built assume we are rational satisfaction-maximisers with perfect knowledge. As irrational human beings with imperfect knowledge, however, our choices are affected by myriad social and psychological factors that do not resemble a calculated cost–benefit analysis. We become who we are with and through others and the biggest influence on our own behaviour is usually the behaviour of our peers as well as our own previous behaviour rather than rational analysis. And often this is for the better, saving us time and freeing us from the burden of solving many problems from scratch. Enormous progress has been made in recent years in the social sciences in such fields as behavioural economics, network theory, game theory and evolutionary psychology. Businesses today need frameworks that can help them engage with people in ways that take creative account of this fresh insight into true human decision-making and behaviour. And these may be unlikely to come from financiers.

Is strategy ripe for re-invention?

Despite the analysis outlined above, the idea of creating Competitive Advantage is still at the front of leaders' minds today around the world. Ask any CEO how he intends to compete and he will give you a ready-made answer. As of today, if you type in the keywords 'competition' and 'business' into Amazon's book search, 13,646 results come up. But is the foundation on which the concept of creating Competitive Advantage is built still solid? After an earthquake hits a city built on sandy, wet or soft clay soils, many of the buildings may at first appear to remain standing as if nothing had happened. Yet underneath them the ground has become deeply insecure. The geological term for this is to say the foundations have become 'thixotropic'. The buildings are no longer safe to use and to ignore this fact puts all of the occupants in danger.

. . . .

Despite the criticism, no alternatives could be embedded in a paradigm as clear, compelling and intuitively right as the concept of creating Competitive Advantage . . . until now?

. . . .

Kiechel's *The Lords of Strategy* tells the story of strategic consulting as practised since its inception in the 1960s and essentially explores the history of competitive strategy through the lens of its leading theorists and practitioners. But what fascinated me most about the book was an admission made in an almost throwaway line in the final chapter that brings the basis of the entire industry into question, challenging the basic assumption on which it has been built: 'The tightly bounded company so long at the core of strategy's deliberations increasingly seems a limited assumption. The twenty-first century version of the discipline will have to do more to help if, or when, the dominant verb becomes not *compete* but something like *co-create*.'*

In many ways this book can be read as an answer to that challenge.

Quick review

- Using competition as a metaphor for business can lead to counter-productive goals and approaches, such as simply trying to offer 'more for less'.

- Models of Competitive Advantage may understate the role that creativity and influence can play in unlocking business value.

- The greatest market disruptions may not come from your apparent competitors but from elsewhere.

- The length of time for which Competitive Advantage can be maintained appears to be diminishing.

- The concept of Competitive Advantage does not provide an adequate explanation for the explosion of collaborative business models or the growth of the sharing economy.

* Kiechel, op. cit., 323.

- Models of Competitive Advantage do not integrate a true understanding of how people make decisions.

- And these models are based on a flawed assumption that the business is a bounded entity that creates value predominantly through internal processes alone.

CHAPTER FOUR

Long live Collaborative Advantage!

Changing opportunities and expectations

In the twentieth century, Competitive Advantage may have stemmed from restricted access to knowledge and resources. Intermediaries such as high-street travel agents had access to information (flight bookings) and privileged access to customers (high-street shoppers, achieved through prime site rental) and made their money by taking their middlemen's fees. Universities educated the elite behind closed doors with knowledge that was unavailable elsewhere. Manufacturers used capital-intensive machinery to produce goods on a scale that prohibited new market entrants.

But is the twenty-first century shaping up to be sufficiently different to merit re-framing the whole goal of doing business and moving on from the incumbent goal of creating Competitive Advantage? Could framing strategy in that way be as out of date as the idea that the only way to gain knowledge is to walk to a reference library?

If business in the twentieth century was about dominating restricted channels of access to knowledge and the means of production in the pursuit of Competitive Advantage, in the twenty-first century these channels are potentially open to anyone with access to the internet and its new means of production. Successful innovation increasingly now derives less from the individually minded pursuit of Competitive Advantage and more from a coalition of the willing to create shared value.

If you attended a party and demonstrated through your actions that your sole goal was not only to eat as much of the food and drink as possible, but specifically to eat and drink more than any of the other guests, leaving the now impoverished party with dwindling provisions, your chances of a second invitation might be slim. If the twenty-first century party is on a global scale then the guests are not just your customers – invitations are extended to at least the three billion people with access to the global conversation of the internet and a chance to influence and to innovate – on their own behalf and on behalf of the four billion who are not yet connected. We face inequality, resource depletion and the suffering associated with complex emergencies, climate change and an accumulation of ever more pressing social challenges. Diminishing our shared resources while offering no true value creation risks retaliation on a scale that no organisation may be able to resist for long.

My hope is that the most successful leaders in the twenty-first century will be those who accurately read the mood and the needs of their audiences, customers and society and provide genuine opportunities to improve people's lives.

A radical alternative

While the story of Competitive Advantage may have helped businesses all around the world to achieve growth from the 1960s, I believe that it is now time to change the story of strategy to support the kind of growth our businesses will be best placed to build now and in the decades to come.

The idea of Competitive Advantage is built on the assumption that the individual organisation is a closed entity and that the value it creates is generated by the careful control of resources that it owns and manages. It was developed in response to the pressing awareness of the arrival of a much greater degree of competitiveness as markets opened up and entrants from other countries started to appeal to previously loyal customers.

....

Collaborative Advantage better supports and activates the true nature of the value-creation process.

....

Collaborative Advantage, however, recognises that value can also be created anywhere in the eco-system in which a business operates. It is a concept developed at a time of increased interconnectedness in which a much broader range of people and organisations outside the business become relevant as possible allies, with the potential to co-create, advocate and scale the business's offerings. From the perspective of creating Collaborative Advantage, organisational success is born out of fostering an optimal relationship with the entire external environment that maximises the combined total value-creating process and generates benefits for the organisation, further enhancing the lives of the customers it serves.

Collaborative Advantage is an inherently optimistic concept. As strategy, innovation and marketing become more open and tie more deeply into our innate capacity for collaboration, I believe organisations can be more successful by engaging greater support and also contribute more to society by reflecting a broader range of needs.

This positive conclusion appears to open the door to a world of business activity that touches us more deeply and does more to improve the lives of the people it serves, as well as create greater financial and other rewards for its owners and employees. It can resolve the dichotomy between giving and taking and implies that the best way to achieve private success is through the creation of public good, aligning the interests of shareholders with broader stakeholders and ushering in more inclusive approaches to business.

Increasing numbers of people and organisations today are already doing more to harness our essential interconnectedness, recognising as a basic starting point that, no matter who you are, there is more talent and resource outside your organisation than inside it. They understand that the better you can become at harnessing and working with that external resource to achieve goals that you can share with others, the more success you are likely to achieve.

Such an approach builds business success not by focusing on outperforming rivals but rather by harnessing the fuller value-creating capabilities of the broader external environment. It tells new stories about what we are in the business of doing and unlocks new types of participation that help us achieve our goals.

....

Creating Collaborative Advantage requires a new mind-set, a new set of expectations and a new set of tools.

....

A new mind-set

This shift has profound implications. It can literally change the neurological origins of our thoughts. Tests have shown that when we think collaboratively rather than competitively, we can use different parts of our brains.

Research into the neural bases of cooperation and competition through functional magnetic resonance imaging (fMRI) of brain activity at the Social Cognitive Neuroscience Laboratory at the University of Washington revealed intriguing results. The researchers contended that cooperation and competition are two basis modes of social cognition that require us to monitor our own behaviour as well as that of others and to adopt a specific mental frame through which we evaluate our interaction.

Participants in an experiment to test this hypothesis were given a specially designed computer game to play that could be played in collaboration or in competition with another person. Brain activity was monitored and it was found that distinct regions of the brain were activated in the two modes, notably the inferior parietal and medial prefrontal cortices in the competitive mode and the orbitofrontal cortex in the case of cooperative mode.

Interestingly, the parts of the brain activated by competition are largely stimulated by extrinsic reward, while the parts of the brain activated in cooperative mode are more associated with intrinsic reward and empathy. The ability to perceive and understand the sentiments of others may be an even greater key to success in a more interconnected world.

The findings led the research team to conclude that cooperation is intrinsically a socially rewarding process. The act of collaboration can be an end in its own right, generating its own side benefits independently of its explicit objectives. It represents a radically different mind-set to competition in the way we monitor activity among our peers, develop a new course of action or change our current planned activity in response to a new social situation.

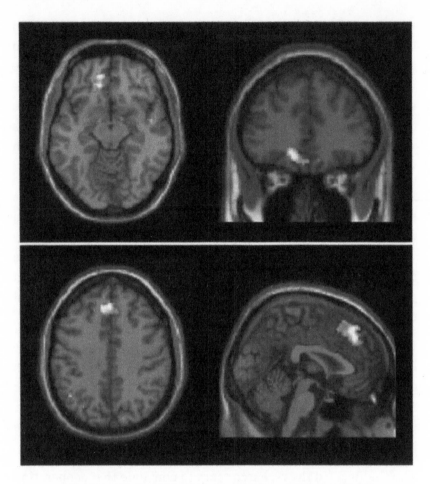

The Neural Bases of Cooperation and Competition: An fMRI
Investigation, Jean Decety, Philip L. Jackson, Jessica A. Sommerville,
Thierry Chaminade and Andrew Meltzoff, *Neuroimage.*
Above: A cooperative brain. Below: A competitive brain.

More broadly, fMRI scanning has greatly increased our understanding of empathy, another key component of a mind-set ready to create
Collaborative Advantage. In his book *The Empathy Instinct,*[*] Peter

---

[*] Peter Bazalgette, *The Empathy Instinct: How to Create a More Civil Society*
(London: John Murray, 2017).

Bazalgette argues that before long we may see brain scanning for our relative capacity for empathy as part of the recruitment process for key jobs in areas such as medicine, with different specialisations better matching different degrees of empathy. I would argue that people in leadership, in externally facing roles and in roles in disciplines such as marketing can also benefit from a well-developed sense of empathy. Many of the best business insights, product innovations and marketing ideas have come from a keen sense of the experience of the customer, the challenges they face and what is most important to them. Empathy can drive a leadership style that seeks to use influence to get the most out of people rather than use force to get the bare minimum.

Speaking about Collaborative Advantage at the Global Meeting of the Women's Forum for the Economy and Society in 2016, I was asked if women are better at creating Collaborative Advantage than men. I hedged my bets at the time, arguing that this may plausibly be the case but that I wasn't qualified to give a definitive answer. According to Bazalgette, however, the balance of evidence so far certainly indicates a greater capacity for empathy among women.

We can nevertheless all further develop a collaborative mind-set simply by tapping into innate capacities that are available to anyone. Every day that passes seems to bring with it new research findings into human cognitive functioning. Many of the insights of this research progressively reveal just how deeply ingrained in our nature our capacity for cooperation may be. As one example, our very capacity for reasoning is now starting to be understood to have evolved primarily to provide a shared currency of persuasion to enable people to reach consensus through conversation. This would explain why not many of us would have the aptitude to sit down alone and write an entire philosophical treatise, but we do generally feel we understand something

better once we've had the chance to talk it through with other
people.*

Changed assumptions

Changing the way we think also means changing the frameworks or
tacit assumptions by which we formulate strategy.

While Competitive Advantage has been the cornerstone of what business schools, professional organisations and thought-leaders have
taught practitioners for decades, we have seen that in today's context
these models just don't deliver the results that they used to. But while
changing the frameworks we know we are using can be hard enough,
the challenge of unpicking our latent assumptions and beliefs can be
even greater. As Keynes wrote in the *General Theory of Employment,
Interest and Money*:

'The ideas of economists and political philosophers – both when they
are right and when they are wrong – are more powerful than is
commonly understood. Indeed, the world is ruled by little else.
Practical men, who believe themselves to be quite exempt from any
intellectual influences, are usually slaves of some defunct economist.'†

Unless we actively create a new narrative to help us understand the
work of formulating strategy, we may be held back by the limitations
of a story that no longer holds true. Unless we consciously formulate
our strategy with the purpose of creating Collaborative Advantage, we
may be unconsciously restricted by the limitations of the idea of
building Competitive Advantage.

* See for example Dan Sperber and Hugo Mercier, *The Engima of Reason: A
New Theory of Human Understanding* (London: Allan Lane, 2017).
† Keynes, op. cit.

Removing the upper limit on success

The shift to the creation of Collaborative Advantage is also exciting in that it can remove the upper ceiling on what we can achieve. By better leveraging external resources, organisations of all sizes can achieve a level of success that is disproportionate to their internal resources. Traction in the marketplace can be more a question of creativity and ideas than budgets and media spend.

While many of the greatest digital campaigns, for example, have been run by major global corporates with extremely deep pockets, others have been run by ordinary people with zero media spend but a highly engaging idea. You may remember an early instance of this in the Facebook campaign run by Jon Morter. Jon was an everyday music fan who was tired of *The X Factor* securing the UK Christmas No. 1 each year and in 2009 he initiated the Rage Against the Machine for Christmas No. 1 campaign and defeated the marketing might of *X Factor* to take the band to the top of the charts. The campaign began with a single posting on Facebook that read: 'Fed up of Simon Cowell's latest karaoke act being Christmas No. 1? Me too . . . So who's up for a mass-purchase of the track "Killing in the Name" from 13 December . . . as a protest to the *X Factor* monotony?'

We live at a time where the potential to reach others with the power of our ideas is perhaps greater than at any previous time in history. As the Rage Against the Machine campaign shows, this can be a lot of fun. As some of the case studies featured later in the book will reveal, this can also be a great opportunity to re-shape the world around us for the better in the most useful and interesting ways we can imagine.

We all see how quickly content can be shared through digital communications and how rapidly new platforms can take off. It is incredible to think how quickly businesses such as Google, Facebook, Twitter,

Uber and Airbnb rose to prominence – and perhaps more so to reflect on how early a stage of the digital revolution we are still in and how much further change lies ahead.

Innovation ex machina

Collaborative Advantage is a concept that can unlock success for organisations of any size. I explored the concept in conversation with my collaborator Roy Sandbach OBE. We realised that we had each been on the journey that ran from creating Competitive Advantage to instead creating Collaborative Advantage albeit in very different contexts. One of my early experiences deploying the concept involved showing how it can work with literally zero budget, while Roy had experienced applying it in a programme that contributed to doubling the size of one of the largest organisations in the world.

Roy held a leadership role in implementing one of the largest collaborative innovation projects in the history of business: the Connect and Develop programme at Procter & Gamble. Connect and Develop was created as part of an intention to make P&G the most collaborative business in the world. They had eight thousand research-and-development staff but knew that there were around two million people in the world working on activities that were relevant to P&G's business needs. As Roy puts it, 'The Connect and Develop programme has been about accessing those people fairly and with a collaborative mind-set.'

It was created in response to the objective set by new CEO A. G. Lafferty to source fifty per cent of P&G's innovation from outside the company. That target was exceeded by a further ten to twenty per cent while Roy was still with the programme. Roy explains, 'It required a clear mandate from the top of the organisation. And it required building an open culture across the organisation, rewarding people for open collaboration and not just for the selfish pursuit of advantage for P&G alone. It involved hiring people with open and connected mind-sets. And it involved a persistent effort to become the sort of partner you would want to work with.'

My experience in creating Collaborative Advantage includes operat-ing at the other end of the business spectrum, building on a start-up voluntary project from scratch. As a marketer I'd often enjoyed offer-ing my marketing skills pro bono to causes that I believed in, but I also noticed that most of my opportunities to do that had come about in somewhat random ways. So I began to wonder whether I might make a more useful contribution by creating a way to enable marketers right across the profession to access that kind of opportunity more efficiently and more systematically. So I developed a platform called Pimp My Cause that works rather like online dating, but connecting professional marketers to small charities and social enterprises to fall in love with. I had literally no budget at all to do it – but that simple change of focus from what I could deliver myself to what I could support others in achieving took my interest in harnessing the power of marketing for good to places I couldn't have imagined before I began.

In the second week the platform was live, a heritage museum in Vancouver connected through the platform with the marketing direc-tor of an auctioneer. They had exactly the expertise and insight the museum needed and were also based in Vancouver, a city that I've never had the pleasure of even visiting. And that unexpected match set the tone for the years which have followed, during which Pimp My Cause has gone on to support over two thousand charities and social enterprises, with well over five million pounds of pro bono marketing, creating over twenty million pounds of social value. Pimp My Cause has members in over thirty countries with over a hundred streams of marketing in progress at any point in time. This is made possible by people and organisations outside the boundaries of our control but whom we can reach and influence, including many top brands and agencies as well as the leading marketing professional organisations.

Working to support thousands of marketing professionals in using their skills to help re-shape the world around us for the better has opened an invaluable window on the possibilities of embedding influence at the heart of strategy. It has inspired much of my thinking in the development of the Collaborative Advantage concept and myriad opportunities to test and improve new approaches.

The Agency of the Future

My first conversations about creating the Agency of the Future were with Lynne Franks OBE. Lynne founded what became the world-famous Lynne Franks PR when she was twenty-one years old. She further came to attention for inspiring the satirical character Edina Monsoon in *Absolutely Fabulous*. Unlike Edina, however, Lynne has real substance with a plethora of achievements, from founding London Fashion Week and putting the UK at the forefront of world fashion to more recently driving some of the most important approaches to the empowerment of women and more sustainable ways of working. She is one of those rare people who can make all things seem possible.

Lynne asked me what an Agency of the Future would look like. Having thought about it I replied that it would be network-based rather than bricks-and-mortar; that it would have an ethical approach to business embedded across all its services rather than as a separate sideline; and that it would undertake its own initiatives as well as serving client organisations. Lynne pointed out that this matched the way I was already working and the idea of launching the Agency of the Future started to take shape.

By the time I launched it, however, I had started to understand its name in a different way. My thoughts on Collaborative Advantage led me to reflect on the other meaning of the word 'agency': taking action to get things done. I realised that the way outcomes can be achieved was changing and that creating Collaborative Advantage was the 'agency' of the future in that second sense of a new way of achieving outcomes through mechanisms of influence and collective participation rather than through control and isolated action.

Running the Agency of the Future has been an ideal complement to the many invaluable lessons I've learned from the inspiring cause leaders and marketers of Pimp My Cause. Through the Agency of the Future I've had the opportunity to support CEOs and leadership teams from start-ups to global corporates and institutions of international cooperation such as the United Nations. We work out how they can harness the power of Collaborative Advantage to achieve their strategic goals. Many of the examples that we'll explore in Parts Two and Three of this book are outcomes of this collaboration.

. . . .

Today's practitioner lacks the availability of a holistic framework for systematically building the alternative to Competitive Advantage. Outside In is intended to fill that gap.

. . . .

A new framework for success

Many organisations are already pioneering ways of creating value that go way beyond anything described in the traditional approaches to competitive strategy. A gap I've identified through my work is that today's practitioner lacks a holistic framework for systematically building the alternative to Competitive Advantage. What is needed is a model for building Collaborative Advantage that can be used to channel the powerful drivers re-shaping the world around us into coherent and integrated strategies for success. And such a model should be capable of being applied in any context.

Part Two will present the Outside In framework in depth. The framework is intended to address this need and I invite you to apply it to your own business activities to maximise the Collaborative Advantage you can build.

Outside In can be applied to re-imagine the structure and function of any organisation, initiative or campaign as a platform for open participation, in order to maximise the opportunities for creating Collaborative Advantage. This usually involves telling a different story about what the organisation exists to achieve and framing new customer and stakeholder propositions accordingly. It can be applied to define organisational purpose, to develop an innovation pipeline, engage with customers and other stakeholders, foster continuous improvement over time and to drive rapid growth.

The approach amounts to a fundamental re-imagination of organisational strategy, which replaces traditional concepts of Competitive Advantage with a contemporary approach to creating Collaborative Advantage.

Collaborative Advantage and the bottom line

Before we move on to working with the Outside In framework in depth in Part Two, it may be worth highlighting some of the key benefits to the bottom line that this approach can be used to enable.

These benefits include:

- Bringing clarity of purpose to galvanise everyone in the organisation and to mobilise partners, collaborators, customers and other stakeholders.

- De-coupling the potential for growth from the limitations of current resources by creating value through mechanisms of influence as well as control.

- Better leveraging the influence and assets of a broader range of stakeholders and contributors.

- Improving the capability to respond positively to surprising events and opportunities.

- Identifying disruptive business models.

- Accelerating the processes of learning, innovation and growth.

- Overcoming dependence on a potentially linear, expensive and rigid internal value chain.

- Lowering the cost of customer recruitment through more positive peer-to-peer influence and by making marketing activity more directly useful and less costly.

- Lowering the cost of customer retention through increased customer participation and loyalty.

- Increasing customer satisfaction, customer loyalty and customer lifetime value by working with customers as active participants in the business.

- Reducing the cost of innovation and increasing its success rate by working with the people it is intended to serve.

- Building more ambitious partnerships.

The overall impact on the bottom line of building Collaborative Advantage and achieving these benefits can be to increase the net present value of future cash-flow. This is the metric used by financiers to measure the total value of a business.[*] And this can be achieved because the approach of building Collaborative Advantage better supports and activates the true nature of the value creation process. Competitive Advantage was born from a classical view of value creation as a linear, enclosed process that is now giving way to an alternative understanding of how value is truly created through more complex, evolutionary and unbounded processes[†] that can better be harnessed by creating Collaborative Advantage.

Whether it is through participatory mapping and mobile payments driving disaster relief and international development, free access to knowledge and open courseware driving the change from education and training to lifelong learning or open innovation systems and new forms of consumer engagement driving the future of business and marketing, organisational success is coming to rely ever more heavily on becoming more open, collaborative and participatory.

Indeed, I would argue that new approaches to collaboration in an increasingly interconnected world already represent the single most powerful driver of change in organisational strategy.

Quick review

- Where concepts of Competitive Advantage are based on creating value by controlling the resources you own and manage,

---

[*] The net present value (NPV) or net present worth (NPW) is a measurement of the profitability of an undertaking that is calculated by subtracting the present values (PV) of cash outflows (including initial cost) from the present values of cash inflows over a period of time.
[†] See for example Eric D. Beinhocker, *The Origin of Wealth: Evolution, Complexity and the Radical Remaking of Economics* (Boston: Harvard Business School Press, 2006).

Collaborative Advantage seeks instead to enable the greatest total value-creating potential by harnessing customers and other stakeholders as key supporters, contributors and agents of the value-creation process.

- Creating Collaborative Advantage requires a new mind-set, a new set of core assumptions and new models of value-creation.

- Collaborative Advantage can be created by businesses of all sizes and can remove the upper limit on success by de-coupling the potential for growth from the level of resource owned by the business.

- Collaborative Advantage reverses the assumption that a business is a bounded entity that creates value through internal processes alone.

- It views business success as the product of an optimal relationship with the entire external environment.

- Creators of Collaborative Advantage can increase business value by building clarity of purpose, accessing external resource to drive growth, enabling a better response to a changing environment, identifying disruptive business models, lowering costs, increasing customer value and building more ambitious partnerships.

PART TWO: HOW?

Using Outside In to create Collaborative Advantage

CHAPTER FIVE

Introducing Outside In

In Part One we explored the rationale for building Collaborative Advantage as a radical alternative to Competitive Advantage. I argued that building Collaborative Advantage is a better fit with our contemporary world than traditional forms of Competitive Advantage and that it holds the key to unlocking vast additional business success with the chance of improving the world around us at the same time. This was based on the observation that while creating Competitive Advantage is a process of using the resources you own, manage and control to create a superior offering, creating Collaborative Advantage is in contrast a process of bringing the fuller value-creating potential of the outside world into the organisation, working with others to achieve greater goals than can be achieved using internal resources alone.

Collaborative Advantage can help us increase our revenues, grow our businesses, improve our innovation, products and services, and open the doors to new partnerships. It can help us stand out in a crowded environment by better working across all the stakeholders present in that environment.

So how can we go about building it in the most systematic way?

Through my own experiments running Pimp My Cause and through my advisory work running the Agency of the Future, I've developed a five-part framework that can be used to re-imagine the structure and function of any organisation, programme, initiative or campaign as a platform for external participation that can be used to maximise the creation of Collaborative Advantage.

This involves taking a systematic approach that moves away from using your own enclosed, owned, controlled resources alone to directly achieve your goals and towards an open model where your internal resources are primarily used as an enabling platform, not designed to do the work in isolation, but rather to make sure the work gets done. It is a framework I have used to build my own businesses and to help clients from start-ups to global corporates to address their own most pressing business challenges. The next five chapters present each step of Outside In and collectively enable you to maximise the Collaborative Advantage that you can create.

One of the most valuable things we can do to improve our development of strategy is to ask ourselves the most useful possible questions. A key challenge, however, is that most of the questions we ask ourselves implicitly take our current assumptions as a starting point. The Outside In framework is intended as a tool to help you overcome that challenge. It is accompanied by a strategic audit designed to further support you in unlocking fresh thinking in the creation of Collaborative Advantage.

The questions in the strategic audit can be found at the end of each chapter in this part of the book and can be applied to your own activities, to the activities you run within your organisation or to your organisation as a whole. This book is not complete without your answers. Indeed, my hope is to help you fill these pages with the basis for a new level of success for yourself, your business and the people your business serves by turning your own activities Outside In.

The Outside In framework and the accompanying strategic audit will help you think differently about the organisation you run or the activities you lead and to see new possibilities for action as a result. As a word of caution I'd say that when these models are adopted, they can be highly disruptive. And although we can decide whether or not to adopt them ourselves, there is nothing we can do to stop others from adopting them and re-writing the rules of our sectors.

While some people may feel excited by the ideas presented, others may feel daunted. There is also still scepticism in some sectors from incumbents who may feel that these kinds of approaches are not something they need to worry about. I participated in a conference hosted by Google for the humanitarian sector and one of the speakers from a large non-governmental organisation struggling with these issues put it very poignantly. He said, 'We don't want to be left behind and become like high-street travel agents or the record industry – sectors that still exist and are sort of doing their thing, but becoming increasingly irrelevant and increasingly marginalised.'

Even so, whether we want to take these kinds of approach or not, we have to look at how they could transform our sectors to be prepared for the changes they can bring with them. The army has a phrase to describe their emphasis on preparedness and risk prevention in turbulent environments – they call it 'getting left of the bang', in the sense of intervening before disruption hits.

I hope that at the very least taking some time to think about some of these issues and what their consequences could be can help us all to get left of the bang.

CHAPTER SIX

Step One: find common purpose

OUTSIDE IN

Step One of Outside In is to find common purpose. It is the most crucial and the most fundamental Step. It consists of identifying what it is that you enable people to do better, framing it in a way that is attractive for them to get involved and orientating your whole organisation around enabling this pursuit. This step includes the creation of a powerful call to action and provides the seed of a new story that will ultimately re-define what your organisation is, why it exists and the contribution it can make to the lives of its customers and other stakeholders. It can provide a foundation for restoring human purpose to your organisation's strategy and for harnessing our innate capacity for cooperation as a means to fulfilling that purpose.

Brand agenda versus brand identity

If a brand identity defines who you are, a brand agenda defines what you enable your customers to do. It is worth remembering, after all, that it is customers who usually create most of the value associated with a purchase. If two people meet in Starbucks for coffee, for example, it is almost certain that their conversation will be more valuable than the cappuccino that accompanies it.

Defining a brand agenda and building your strategy around it can be thought of as a radical alternative to the kinds of approaches to brand development that predominated in the 1980s and 1990s. These approaches largely involved defining your positioning or the identity or image of your brand and mobilising most internal activity around that. The aim was to ensure that this image would be effectively communicated in every point of contact with your audience and nothing that you did would deviate from this position.

So, for example, in the early days of my career at L'Oréal, a nightmare scenario might have involved the marketing team in Spain selling our Kérastase brand with promotional gifts that didn't fit with the Kérastase image or the marketing team in Greece selling Kérastase at a price that did not match the international recommendation that reflected that image. The grandfather of branding, Wally Olins, who pioneered branding as a discipline in its own right, undertook his first business development work by going into companies with printouts of all of the discrepancies between the way they communicated their identity in different places as his sales pitch for why they needed his services.*

In building Collaborative Advantage, businesses still need a strong brand identity, but that identity no longer provides the organising principle of strategy. Rather, it has a different contribution to make. From the perspective of creating Collaborative Advantage, the most important facet of a brand is its ability to lower the threshold to external participation in the pursuit the business exists to enable in the first place. To achieve this a brand must be memorable, salient and attractive to the people you seek to involve.

We each make thousands of choices a day but our lives do not grind to a halt partly because simple, usually unconscious heuristics appear to guide most of these choices, keeping them easy to make: usually 'What did I do last time? And what do most other people do?'

A strong brand identity can lower the threshold to customer participation in the brand agenda by making it easier for people to remember the brand and easier to spot other people using it. A compelling brand identity can also play a useful role in supporting a sense of belonging that can further enhance the process of participation by giving people an opportunity to participate alongside others with whom they like the opportunity to be associated.

. . . .

Step One plants the seed of a new story that will ultimately re-define what your organisation is, why it exists and what it enables the world to do better.

. . . .

* Wally Olins, *Brand New: The Shape of Brands to Come* (London: Thames & Hudson, 2014).

A brand agenda complements the brand identity by carefully framing the particular activity, pursuit or enthusiasm that you seek as a brand to empower other people to enjoy participating in. And in so doing it provides a call to action that, from the perspective of creating Collaborative Advantage, should replace brand identity as the organising basis for your marketing activity and your strategy. It asks you to base your strategy less on who you are and more on what you enable your customers and other stakeholders to do better.

Identifying the right brand agenda can help you create the right identity to adopt to begin with. For example, I worked recently with an agency that provides analysis and evaluation of crises and disasters for the humanitarian sector. We defined their brand agenda in the compelling call to action, 'See the crisis. Change the outcome'. This works as a brand agenda, focusing on the improved humanitarian outcomes they can help users of their information services to achieve in terms of ultimately changing the trajectory of crises for the better, protecting life and alleviating suffering. It also gives the agency more space to think not just about the information and evaluation they provide, but how they can ensure that their analysis can be made as actionable as possible in the context in which it is used. And finally, it opened the door to a conversation about a new identity capable of serving this brand agenda. At first we considered 'Humanitarian Eyes' for its obvious connection to the theme of seeing crises better as an enabler to providing a better response. But that identity had the risk of implying a type of surveillance that bore no relation to the agency's activities, so instead we settled on the wordplay-based 'Crisis in Sight', which still foregrounds the fact that they bring disasters into focus, but with a greater emphasis on their provision of non-obvious, actionable insights that can support responders in taking better decisions.

Brand agenda for start-ups

A further example reveals the significance of what otherwise may seem an abstract shift away from placing your identity at the heart of your strategy towards using an agenda or external stakeholder pursuit as the organising principle of your business.

A group of sustainability professionals, including my friends John Grant and Ayça Apak Tonge, looked at the consulting sector in their field of expertise and ended up launching an intriguing initiative that had an early influence on the development of my thinking on Collaborative Advantage. They wanted to re-invent the model of sustainability consulting services, in which consultants go into client companies to identify eco-efficiency savings. A perfectly good business perhaps, but one that doesn't necessarily come across as exciting, so they thought it might be ripe for re-invention. They saw that underlying the model of sustainability consulting was an interest in preserving the environment by using fewer resources – or as they put it 'making the most of using less'. That's something anyone can join in with, and that conceptually different starting point allowed them to create a new business model.

They developed a social networking platform called ecoinomy, based on a concept called 'fund-saving' as an alternative to fundraising that can be deployed in client organisations to empower their own staff to identify eco-efficiency savings within the remit of their own jobs and to incentivise the system by splitting the financial value of those savings between the client and the charities of each employee's choosing. Everyone wins because the total efficiency savings become so much greater when you effectively get everyone on board. Ecoinomy enabled a win for the environment, a win for client businesses and a win for the employees and their favourite community projects.

The approach involved understanding the firm in a different way and taking radically different action as a result. It was a move away from 'We are the experts' and 'We provide the answers' to 'We enable you to make the changes you want to achieve'. The simple act of defining a brand agenda, in this case 'Making the most of using less' planted the seed of a new story – a way of understanding the line of business the firm was in – and marked the birth of a new strategy that could successfully build Collaborative Advantage by unlocking the active and collective participation of the very people the firm was intended to support.

That sounds a lot more interesting than traditional sustainability consulting to me – and Deborah Meaden from *Dragons' Den* obviously agreed, as she became an investor and the company chairman.

So a subtle or conceptual shift in our starting point away from a focus on ourselves and towards the interest that we can foster can lead to a radically different approach based on a completely new set of assumptions.

Brand agenda for global brands

Many of the world's greatest brands across all parts of the economy have adopted such an approach, framing our own active participation as users in their key propositions in inspiring ways.

We could think of Wikipedia, its approach implicit in everything it does, to support contributors in making all knowledge available to everyone everywhere for free: a truly galvanising pursuit and one that has evolved into a highly sophisticated and codified process that has grown organically from the collective learning and collaboration of contributors. Or Nike's invitation to 'Just do it' and get actively involved in sport the world over: a pursuit that we'll come back to in Step Two of the framework.

When the ad agency St Luke's was asked to boost the restaurant chain Harvester's brand they took a similar approach, based around the theme 'Harvester: bring out the best', inviting customers not just to enjoy the food, but to enjoy time together with friends or family that celebrates the best of our shared time with the people closest to us. One of the most universal and recognisable examples is Coca-Cola's brand agenda of enjoying a refreshing moment of happiness. At times this has been expressed as 'Enjoy', 'Open happiness' or 'Choose happiness'. That was relevant in 1931 when Coca-Cola introduced the world to a vision of Santa Claus as a large, jolly man in a red suit with a white beard. And it is the driving force of Coke's marketing inspiration around the world to this day. I remember Jonathan Mildenhall, at the time Coca-Cola's vice-president of advertising, telling me that for Coke, the competition isn't the 'liquid in the blue bottle', but is rather other brands inviting us to enjoy a moment of happiness, such as McDonald's or Disneyland.

It would be easy to be cynical about these kinds of optimistic propositions. A Coke can't really make you happy after all, right? But in the end it is we who use them as consumers who create their real meaning in our lives. When my father first saw Coke bottles with names on them, he bought one with my name on it ahead of my visit to my parents at their home in Aylesbury. There is something joyful about seeing our own name or the name of someone we love on a bottle. On that occasion, sadly, the visit ended up instead being to the hospital where he had been unexpectedly admitted in emergency and my father never made it back to the house to give me the bottle himself. But I keep it to this day as his last little gift to me. The meaning we build around brands can be very real.

I serve on the advisory board of the Museum of Brands, Packaging and Advertising in London, and walking through the museum's Time Tunnel, with its treasure trove of branded goods from hundreds of years ago to the present day, I've noticed that the exhibits that get the most attention are invariably the brands of our childhoods. And the number one topic of conversation is remembering with surprise and affection the things we did while using those brands – the games we played, the relationships we enjoyed and the times we lived through. The more a brand can orientate itself around the things it enables its customers to do, the more strongly it can harness that power as a basis for growth.

I was involved in developing a brand-training programme for Sony Mobile at a time when they were changing their approach to their Xperia brand to make it less about the brand and more about what the user can do with the brand, with the brand agenda tagline, 'Making the everyday extraordinary'. Of course it wasn't Sony making the everyday extraordinary, it was Sony's customers who were enabled by Xperia to do that for themselves in new and interesting ways. And this agenda became the new organising principle for the brand, with a new approach to communications that focused on what each aspect of an Xperia device enabled the user to do.

This has similarities with a recent campaign developed by IBM under the banner 'You^{IBM}'. Early propositions associated with this campaign include the claim, 'While no human alone can read, see, feel, hear and make sense of all the data transforming your profession, IBM Cloud with Watson can enable you to better do your life's work.'[*]

Fundamental differences of customer purpose can also explain how apparently similar businesses differentiate themselves. Let's take two leading online video platforms for example: YouTube and Vimeo. While offering apparently similar propositions at a superficial level, in reality they have targeted very different core user purposes. YouTube has enabled anyone to be a creator and has democratised the process of

[*] www.ibm.com/thought-leadership/you

uploading and viewing content by making it as easy as possible in order to achieve the greatest possible reach. Vimeo, on the other hand, has concentrated on providing tools that enable quality production and playback for skilled and professional users who already have their audiences and are seeking above all to control quality.

On purpose

In Part One we explored how a strong sense of purpose is increasingly being identified as a key driver of organisational success. Indeed, a study conducted by EY, assessing over five hundred companies, found that a clearly defined and mobilising purpose correlated with improved business performance against every metric they could measure.[*] Purposeful organisations and brands can have more engaged and loyal employees and customers, can be more innovative and profitable and can sustain these advantages over the long term. 'Purpose' has found a new zeitgeist in the business world and made it back to the top of leaders' priorities. But few people have defined what they mean by 'purpose' and fewer still have asked the question 'Whose purpose is it anyway?'

A brand agenda can provide a powerful means to cultivate a strong sense of purpose where it matters most – in the minds and behaviours of customers. When you can unite your customers around the pursuit of your brand agenda, you can unlock myriad ways to involve them more deeply, loyally and sociably in all your propositions.

This outward-looking approach to purpose can also enable people inside the business to better understand and deliver on their own roles. I've often found in my own client work that beginning with a

---

[*] *The Business Case for Purpose*, a 2015 Harvard Business Review Analytic Services report.

focus on developing the right brand agenda can play a substantial role in galvanising a whole organisation, helping teams to better understand their own activities in terms of how they enable their customers to improve their own lives as well as the contribution that is made to society through the process. Making the customer the hero of the brand story can play an excellent role in embedding a distinctive customer service ethos across the business in a way that reaches from the shop floor to the chief executive officer.

A focus on underlying purpose rather than simply a set of existing solutions also drives curiosity, experimentation and innovation. It fosters a permanent desire to go beyond existing performance and methods. It can play a crucial human-resource role in providing staff with a true vocation to pursue, unlocking new meaning in their work and drawing out their fullest capacity to contribute.

If a brand agenda provides our story in seed form, we can also build on it to extrapolate a powerful mission and vision for the business. If the brand agenda is what we support our customers in doing, our mission can be framed in terms of how we are going to enable them to do it and our vision can be articulated in terms of what the world looks like when that activity is better enabled. A strong brand agenda gets us off to the best possible start to engaging people in our mission and vision and enables us to mobilise internal and external resources around a single organising thought.

A compelling mission and vision are often already recognised as crucial in the charity world, where organisations spend a lot of time soul-searching when they come to write their statements of purpose and, even more importantly, when they consider how best to fulfil them through all their activities. They are also, however, becoming more urgently relevant to an increasing share of for-profit brands and businesses that see them as a basis for differentiation, engagement and success.

Indeed, we can all do with thinking through how the world could be enhanced by the greater adoption of our products or services – and, if the world wouldn't be better off with more of what we have to offer, then maybe we should question whether we're offering the right proposition in the first place.

A little more action please

The switch from brand identity to brand agenda as the organising principle heralds an opportunity to shift the focus of communications from changing attitudes to changing behaviours.

We tend to believe that our actions follow our beliefs but in reality it's more likely the other way around. We shape our beliefs to justify our actions. Or as Steven Kaas put it in his memorable tweet, 'You are not the king of your brain. You are the creepy guy standing next to the king going, "A most judicious choice, sire".' We may think that we choose brands because we like them, but it may be that the causality is the other way around: we like brands because we have chosen them. And the original choice may simply have been the result of the brand's convenient availability to us. These distortions from purely rational selection are known respectively as a 'confirmation bias' and an 'availability bias' in behavioural economics, the science of human decision-making that we'll come back to in Step Three.

Evidence in the IPA Databank* adds a further dimension by showing that campaigns that set a behavioural objective are more effective than those that set awareness or attitudinal objectives. So when we frame our proposition in terms of what we enable our customers to do, we also open the doors to their liking us more for it in the process. After all, if they like to 'do our thing', it must be for a reason . . .

* www.ipa.co.uk

A powerful evolutionary purpose can bring the fuller capabilities for innovation of the outside world to bear on the growth of an organisation.

One thing leads to another

A strong purpose can also lead to unexpected positive surprises. 'Systems theory' can help us understand patterns of human activity in which one thing leads to another. This explains how customs such as leaving flowers by the roadside after someone is killed in a traffic accident spreads quickly without promotion. We see the gesture made by others and, faced with a similar situation, make the same gesture ourselves. It also illustrates why we no longer understand a market as the aggregation of individuals within the market but rather as the complex product of the interactions between them. People influence each other far more than we influence them.

Our markets and audiences, like any groups of people, can best be understood as 'complex adaptive systems' that can change dramatically as a result of their own internal interactions. They are not like machines that, as the mechanics of a watch, may be 'complicated' but nevertheless follow linear rules and consequently have predictable non-complex outcomes.

One of the greatest contributions a powerful purpose can unlock is that of enabling people and groups outside the business to identify with that purpose and open the doors to new activity and collaboration that could not have been generated from within the organisation itself. When a spider weaves its web in the midday sun, it doesn't know what will come its way. But by weaving its web it maximises its chances of converting unexpected arrivals into lunch. A powerful purpose that people can readily remember and bring to mind puts us in pole position to attract new ideas and opportunities, many of which could in no way have been foreseen by us at the start of the process and which fit with our purpose and help to further support our expanding success (fortunately we can make our lunch *with* our collaborators – we don't have to eat them!).

Such a purpose supports the growth of a business in an evolutionary way by enabling more options for growth to be identified by people inside and outside the business, by providing a mechanism for selecting which of these options for action offers the best fit with what the organisation exists to support people in doing and by providing a focus to enable collaborative support for and participation in the selected options. This can create a much stronger foundation for innovation than can ever be achieved by most companies operating according to outdated models of strategy that view the controlled resources of the business in isolation from the contributions that can be harnessed from the outside world.

Indeed, it is interesting to review research that shows that, typically, innovation does not occur so much within firms as in the spaces between them. Hannan and Freeman's landmark studies on the 'organisational ecology' of markets,[*] for example, suggest that innovation does not primarily take place within individual businesses but primarily at the level of markets overall. Innovation occurs less because existing firms adapt, the research indicates, and more because new firms enter and replace the existing ones. This does not appear to be good news for existing businesses.

A powerful evolutionary purpose, however, can help to overcome this challenge by bringing the full innovation capabilities of the outside world to bear on the growth of an organisation. These can include

---

[*] See, for example, Michael T. Hannan and John Freeman, *Structural Inertia and Organisational Change*, American Sociological Review, April 1984, Vol. 49, No. 2, 149–64.

technology, resources and relationships that otherwise would be beyond the means of the business. It can provide a powerful stimulus to keeping the business in a constant state of dynamic growth, trying new approaches, gathering support for what works and discarding methods that can be surpassed. The individual business may of necessity have a limited supply of talent and resource but can use an evolutionary purpose to attract both from the broader market, from other related markets and even from apparently non-related markets as we'll further review in later chapters.

A Yiddish proverb, once famously glossed by Woody Allen, suggests that if you want to make God laugh, you should tell him your plans for the future. I remember Tim Smit, the founder of the botanical collection the Eden Project telling me, in perhaps a similar spirit, why he doesn't believe in five-year plans. 'There are two types of activity. Things that are worth doing. And things that aren't. If something is not worth doing, don't do it. If it is worth doing, why wait?' And Apple's Steve Jobs was famous for being relentlessly obsessive about purpose, but remaining open-minded about how that purpose might be achieved.

All of this apparently disparate wisdom may appear to draw from a shared understanding. Predicting the terrain of the future is difficult, so having a clear North Star that enables you to wend your way towards your destination as befits the lie of the land is more useful than following a detailed roadmap that will almost certainly turn out to be wrong.

Segmentation by purpose

Using purpose as a tool for planning and for mobilising collective energy inside and outside the business can be further enhanced through processes of segmentation, either by dividing the core brand agenda into constituent segments of activity or by framing goals that can be achieved over time through the pursuit of that activity.

Segmenting a purpose by activity can resemble the process of brand segmentation, through which a parent brand is divided into its constituent sub-brands. Following such an approach the components of an organisation and its customer-facing propositions can be structured around the particular ways in which they each contribute to the overall shared purpose or brand agenda. For example, a humanitarian initiative that I advised developed the brand agenda 'Out-thinking disaster' that could be sub-divided into their three key pillars of activity: 'Learning to out-think disaster', 'Planning to out-think disaster' and 'Working together to out-think disaster'.

If purpose can be segmented horizontally by sub-purpose it can also be segmented vertically over time with stages of accomplishment. Associating specific intended targets with your purpose can play an effective role in galvanising collective progress over a specific time period, fostering an immediate sense of urgency and focus.

Rick Falkvinge, the founder of the Pirate Party in Sweden, knows a thing or two about mobilising participation. He recommends that, in order to inspire mass support, goals should be framed around ideas for change that must be 'tangible, credible, inclusive and epic'.[*] One of the first goals around which he mobilised participation in forming the Pirate Party was to work with the 1.2 million citizens in Sweden who were sharing music, film and other content in infringement of copyright to attempt to amass the 225,000 political votes required to have one member of the party elected to the Swedish parliament.

---

[*] Rick Falkvinge, *Swarmwise: The Tactical Manual to Changing the World* (North Charleston: CreateSpace, 2013).

What surprising results could be achieved if you worked with your customers to build shared objectives around the contribution that you make to their lives?

Giving voice to your people

The French have an expression: *'Penser, c'est vouloir dire. Savoir; c'est pouvoir dire.'* The implication of the phrase is that 'if you can't say it, you can't know it'. While you may have an inkling of something you can't yet find the words to express, there is a sense in which you have to be able to articulate something to be sure you truly know what it is. While a thought can start to emerge before the language to encode it is found, it is not until it can be expressed verbally that it can be fully identified and followed. Language shapes thought and embedding an idea in the right words can better enable its infusion into culture.

One of the most compelling techniques of cooperative leadership consists of reading the latent aspirations of a group and giving voice to those intentions or deeper needs in a way that people 'recognise' when they hear it, almost as if they had been thinking it in advance. In some of the most powerful instances, the proposition can be so strong as to retrospectively appear inevitable – even when in reality it may have been expressed in conditions of the greatest complexity, turbulence and ambiguity.

Calls to action have represented some of the most powerful turning points in world history. Consider the following examples with which you will already be deeply familiar (the emphasis is mine):

'I've seen the promised land. I may not get there with you. But I want you to know tonight, that we, as a people, will **get to the promised land**." Martin Luther King Jr.

* Civil rights speech, 3 April 1968.

69

'We shall **defend our island**, whatever the cost may be, we shall fight on the beaches, we shall fight on the landing grounds, we shall fight in the fields and in the streets, we shall fight in the hills; we shall never surrender.'* Winston Churchill

'And so, my fellow Americans, ask not what your country can do for you, **ask what you can do for your country**. My fellow citizens of the world, **ask** not what America will do for you, but **what together we can do for the freedom of man**.'† John F. Kennedy

These calls to action enable the listener to understand a particular form of action, or collective pursuit, in a particular way, through a particular lens, that is so compelling that if you were among the audience you might well have believed your own sentiment of solidarity, courage or duty had been identified and articulated. They strike an existing chord within you and, through the eloquence of their expression, also chart courses of action that you otherwise would have been unlikely to identify and follow in quite the way expressed. The calls to action that I've placed in bold all appeal to mind and body as one in expressing themselves as invitations to participate in the sensorimotor experiences of arriving, defending and asking respectively. The thought of the speaker overflows into the imagined physical movement of the audience. It is as if the first step of collaboration is taken just by hearing the words.

It is a great thing that few of us are required to engage people with our stories in moments of such collective consequence. But every time we call people to action it can be with an attempt to identify a better path for them to follow, it can elevate their experience in undertaking something of meaning to them and it can be with a purpose that brings us together.

---

* House of Commons speech, 4 June 1940.
† Presidential inaugural address, 20 January 1961.

Quick review

- Step One of Outside In defines a brand agenda or key headline call to action.

- This step re-defines what your business is and what it enables the world to do better. It marks the birth of your strategy to create Collaborative Advantage.

- It also helps you to build corporate purpose by defining your mission and vision in terms of the change you wish to make to your customers' lives and to the world around you.

- It enables you to achieve more efficient and effective marketing that works with the way people take decisions individually and collectively.

- It also helps you to segment your purpose by type of offering and to set exciting goals that involve people in achieving your purpose alongside you.

- It can also be the source of new insight into latent opportunities for growth.

Step One: strategic audit

1 What activity do you enable your customers or beneficiaries to do better?

2 How can this be summarised in a unique proposition? This can become your brand agenda.

3 What role does your organisation play in enabling this activity? This becomes your mission.

4 How would the world be improved by more of this activity? This becomes your vision.

5 What goals can you provide to challenge people inside and outside your organisation to achieve more through common purpose?

6 What identity can you develop to be more salient, memorable and relevant to your brand agenda? This can form your brand identity.

CHAPTER SEVEN

Step Two: create opportunities

OUTSIDE IN

Step Two in the Outside In framework is creating opportunities. This is about designing useful and interesting ways for people to engage in the specific pursuit you have identified and articulated in Step One. Whether you supply products, services or other offerings, what matters most is how people use what you deliver and the role it plays in their lives or work. Enhancing this experience can be a powerful route to success.

Let's get useful

There is a long history of companies inventing or promoting the underlying pursuit that their products support rather than just the products themselves. For example, Nike famously popularised jogging as a form of exercise and used the craze that ensued to sell their early running shoes. Indeed, engaging people in participating in sports first (Nike exists to inspire athletes – claiming that if you have a body, you are an athlete!) and then selling products to them as a by-product of their interest, has continued to be the hallmark of Nike's marketing. Even today, you can buy Nike shirts that have the words 'This is just a shirt' emblazoned across the chest to emphasise the point. But through Nike+, the company has used technology combined with human understanding to take that approach to a new level.

Nike+ brings together a GPS (Global Positioning System) sensor, digital devices (ranging from iPhones to Nike+ watches) and a web platform to allow runners to pursue their 'Just do it' brand agenda in interesting, useful and novel ways. Nike has become a master in creating new ways to enjoy running through Nike+. This essence of the Nike+ brand is to create such opportunities for the growing Nike+ community. These formats include:

• Tracking runs digitally

• Setting private or public goals

• Training with coaches and sports stars

• Monitoring progress on a personal dashboard

- Mapping and sharing runs

- Challenging other runners, both individually and in groups

- Listening to music and sharing running playlists

- Joining Nike+ Run Clubs and participating in sponsored events

This approach reportedly enabled Nike to grow their running shoe market share by ten per cent in the USA while reducing their advertising spend by fifty-five per cent. This is a remarkable achievement for a leading brand in a mature market. And Nike has now added a Nike+ Training Club to their Run Club offering, diversifying the range of activities enabled through an app that gives you access to a wide range of fifteen to forty-five minute workouts led by world class athletes from the comfort of your home, with options to suit people of all levels from newbies to near professionals.

Many marketers may believe that the key to engaging their audiences lies in 'relevant' content. But Nike+ succeeds not by offering 'relevance' but rather by offering 'utility'. And I'd argue that utility beats relevance every time. But while Nike's example is well-known and there are many others, do the vast majority of organisations nevertheless leave on the table the value that their own equivalent to Nike+ could create?

How much success could Hallmark have achieved if they had created Facebook? How much success could Lynx have achieved if they'd invented Tinder? Or how much could Kodak have achieved if they'd been behind Instagram?

Like each of the other steps in the Outside In framework, this step can be applied to organisations at a corporate-wide level and also to individual programmes or even campaigns run by the organisation.

To give an example, the Virgin Media 'Challenge your broadband' campaign was built on the insight that broadband speeds don't really mean anything to people. So to better help people understand the speed improvements they offered, Virgin enabled people to test their broadband with an online speed checker, which then featured Usain Bolt to guide them through the process of switching to Virgin Media if their own broadband failed the challenge. This helped Virgin gain three per cent market share with a significantly lower media spend.

Or if Davina McCall is more your speed, Tesco developed a series of useful adverts for their F&F activewear range. The ads ran during ITV ad breaks in the summer of 2017 and replaced a traditional advert with a short workout routine that viewers could join brand ambassador Davina in performing to get their day off to an accessibly healthy start.

Step Two can also be extended to create opportunities for different groups to come together in ways that create multiple benefits or 'wins' for all parties. This typically involves enabling an exchange of value between different user groups. In these cases where the participants generate the core value themselves, the role of the organisation is to convene, curate and, where necessary, arbitrate, in order to enable optimal exchanges between participants. The key to identifying this kind of opportunity is to find latent value-creating opportunities and exchanges that have hitherto not been accessed at scale, for example by identifying underused assets or capabilities and ways to connect them with people who might be able to benefit from access to them.

Dining, but not as we know it

Grub Club offers people the opportunity to enjoy unique dining experiences that combine a fine meal cooked by an identifiable chef with intriguing one-off venues. These venues are perfect for diners who, in the words of the founder, Olivia Sibony, 'are looking for something different, [and] come to our site in order to enjoy extraordinary meals in curious corners'.*

Grub Club straddles three innovative, growing economies: the 'gig' or 'on-demand economy', where chefs – in this case – make money using their skills in their spare time; the 'experience economy', where diners seek out memorable experiences as the trend increases towards consumers wanting to spend their money on experiences over possessions; and, of course, the 'sharing economy', where owners can hire out their space during their downtime. This enables them to generate extra revenue with no additional workload and for spaces open to the public this has the additional advantage of making the venue known to potential new customers.

The venture also opens the door to new social encounters, as diners have the option of booking alone and joining others on the night on shared tables or participating in options such as the 'literary hour', which combines the appeal of a tasty meal and an inspiring book club. Equally, an increasing number of clients are choosing to take over the entire space in order to have their own private restaurant for the night. Thanks to the efficiency of maximising underused space, the options for diners and chefs are endless and people who own the space no longer have to worry about paying their rent at the end of the month thanks to the increased revenue and footfall.

As Olivia further explains, 'For chefs, this is also a great testing ground for their concept. They can literally set up their own restaurant with little to no upfront capital expenditure. Rather than the current gulf between not owning a restaurant and owning one, this provides the stepping stones towards helping them build their food business without the risks associated with setting up a traditional restaurant.' They may realise over time that owning a restaurant isn't for them and they

* Olivia's comments were made at the Westminster eForum on the Sharing Economy in the UK.

just continue to do this part time, alongside other jobs. Or they may decide that they've found the right formula to set up a restaurant and now have a case study to present to investors which is robust, with a proven concept and existing customers. They also know that they can rent out their space in their downtime, thus minimising financial risk. And, in addition to all this, they are connected through a collaborative community, in which they can learn from each other, find support and work together.

This can also present opportunities for other businesses. Companies including Spotify, Nike and Google have hired out an entire Grub Club in order to take their teams or clients out. This provides a fresh alternative to a traditional restaurant and is a great way to engage their employees or clients in their work, showcasing what they can offer.

Other companies have gone one step further. Wahaca, the Mexican street food chain, use supper clubs as a branding opportunity: every few months, founder Thomasina Miers comes back into the kitchen to cook for her fans, which is something she rarely gets the opportunity to do and is a rare treat for diners. This builds loyalty within their existing customer base, as well as attracting new diners to their restaurant.

Brands have also taken the opportunity to get closer to their customers, with product placement. Peroni created a bespoke sharing menu based around customers' memories of Italy. The whole meal was used as a basis for showcasing a new type of beer that they were launching. The wine shop Borough Wines turns their shop into a restaurant at night: a chef comes in to cook a meal which is specially paired with their wines, so that they can have an opportunity to showcase their wines at their best and sell them to an engaged customer base.

And even charities have found a way to use supper clubs to their advantage. The peace building charity International Alert ran their third year of the Conflict Café at the end of September 2017. Each year, they focus on two to four countries impacted by conflict, where they work. Their aim is to bring about positive discussions around these cultures, in order to celebrate them and change the image of the country. In 2016, one of the countries was Syria. A Syrian chef cooked for the week and, during the meal, diners were able to not only enjoy the amazing food but also hear about the work that the charity does in the country to strive to foster conflict resolution. As a result of this series, the charity has not only raised money, but also received much greater media attention and had the chance to showcase their work in a positive light that makes an encouraging change from the relentlessly bleak messages that we might otherwise hear.

. . . .

What are people doing when they use your products or services? How could you make this experience easier, more enjoyable or more useful?

. . . .

Who is your chief experience officer?

Just as Step One of Outside In encourages us to think not just about who we are, but also more significantly about what we enable people to do better, Step Two asks us to think not just about what we supply, but more importantly about how people can use what we supply.

For an energy company, this might for example be about creating systems that allow people to better understand, measure and manage their use of household electricity. For a bank, this could likely involve programmes to support people in better planning their finances and managing their money. Or a pharmaceutical company could not only supply medication but rather better support patients in choosing and following their treatment options.

As the son of a man who had a heart transplant, I'm intimately aware of the challenges of taking a whole host of delicately balanced and constantly changing medications on a daily basis for an extended period. My father took his 'daily cocktails' religiously, but there are many conditions for which the required self-administration is even more demanding, and huge sums of money can be wasted when pharmaceutical suppliers are paid by healthcare systems for the medicines they supply rather than the medicines that are ultimately correctly taken.

For these reasons, businesses seeking to get on the right side of user participation are increasingly turning to the creation of roles such as chief experience officer or, more commonly, chief customer officer. In the case of pharmaceutical companies, it is the patients themselves whose experience, awareness and potential for participation have been most dramatically affected by the democratisation of healthcare data. Patients and their caregivers are increasingly empowered to participate in decisions regarding the most appropriate choice of therapy to meet their needs. This can lead doctors and other representatives of formal healthcare systems to re-evaluate their prescribed treatments according to a deeper understanding of patient need and preference. Traditionally, the role of the doctor has simply been to extend life, but individual patient preferences concerning the quality of life and willingness to accept risk often need to be taken more meaningfully into account.

How far can this principle be extended? Dr Anne C. Beal is chief patient officer at Sanofi and spoke at the Women's Forum for the Economy and Society at their Global Meeting in 2016 where, as a fellow speaker, I tested some of the material for this book. Anne used her intervention at the conference to explain Sanofi's interest in enhancing patient-centric outcomes, transparency, partnership and continuous learning.

Sanofi uses techniques of creative design to bring patients in to help design clinical protocols and tools such as apps that support people in the self-administration of their medicines. This is particularly important now – whereas a hundred years ago we died primarily of infectious diseases, such as pneumonia, tuberculosis or diarrhoea, today we primarily die of chronic diseases such as heart disease, high blood pressure or diabetes. In the case of infectious disease, the doctor is at the centre of the treatment in administering the appropriate drugs, but in the case of chronic disease, the patient has a far more significant role in terms of making lifestyle changes, thinking about nutrition and monitoring their own progress. As Anne concluded, to enable patients to best address chronic conditions means ensuring they understand their condition, form their own priorities and engage with healthcare providers to jointly achieve the outcomes that mean the most to the patient.

Looking forward, Anne sees the future of participatory healthcare residing largely in prevention. The key challenge that pharmaceutical companies have not yet properly addressed is the business model of how to create what Anne calls a 'never event'. We want people not just to age, but to age well, which requires patient-centric approaches to extending wellness. I wonder whether these models will be developed by pharmaceutical companies themselves or by other groups who have collaborative participation embedded more deeply in their DNA?

Fixing things before they're broken

Insurance is a sector that could arguably be accused of being supply-oriented and transactional. If we were never legally required to buy insurance, we might more often stop and think about the benefits it provides and actively choose to take out cover because it makes good sense to do so. As it stands, however, we mostly buy insurance as an obligation, which means we frequently attempt primarily to minimise the fuss and the price. When Mark Evans took over as marketing director at Direct Line Group, insurance was by tradition marketed entirely around the moment of purchase. Focused on price, consumers overlooked how their insurance will actually perform in the moment of truth when something goes wrong. At their point of need, customers need to be able to carry on with their lives as normally as possible. As Mark explains, 'The category benefit had been hiding in plain sight for many years. Insurance as a sector had largely forgotten that its primary purpose is to fix customers' problems at the point of need. This remarkably simple insight led to the "fixers" campaign that epitomised high performance insurance and turned the brand around, galvanising the whole organisation in the process.'

Direct Line staff are rightly the heroes of the 'fixers' story. They embody the spirit of fixing, frequently going above and beyond the call of duty to help customers to get back on their feet when the worst besets them. And customers have their role to play in carrying on with life that bit more quickly and conveniently as a result. But could there be an even more active role that customers could be supported in playing to make themselves the heroes of the story?

Like Dr Anne Beal, Mark is also a big fan of preventing problems before they occur. That's why, when it was identified that drivers are eight times more likely to kill someone in their first year on the road – and, moreover, that their first thousand miles of driving is a particularly dangerous time when the divergence between perceived and actual driving performance is at its greatest – Direct Line decided to act. In seeking to reduce the number of road deaths in the first thousand miles to zero, the pivotal behavioural insight they identified was that new drivers, particularly young men, considered driving fast to be cool.

It's not easy to change such a deeply embedded pattern of behaviour, but Direct Line found a clever way to make safe driving the appealing thing to do. 'Far too frequently we were seeing tragic stories of young drivers who kill or maim themselves and others very soon after passing their driving test,' says Mark. 'We launched the mobile-only [Direct Line] Shotgun brand to provide safe passage through this vulnerable time. Through gamification that enables friends to compete with each other to be the safest driver, supported by a reward structure based heavily in behavioural economics and a daring style of communication, we have flipped it on its head and made driving safely cool.' This move into the business of prevention is logical for insurers in that it is an act of enlightened self-interest to avoid the cost of serious car accidents but Direct Line go one step further in making this available to all new drivers, not just their own customers, since they can see such a significant societal benefit in so doing.

What might be the ultimate potential of making the customers of insurance policies the heroes of their own lives in preventing problems from occurring in the first place? This is a subject we'll explore with regards to some of the greatest challenges of our time in chapter 12, 'Addressing Global Challenges'.

How much will you play me?

A small town in the mid-west of the USA welcomes visitors with a sign by its principal access road displaying the words, 'Now showing Fairfield: a cast of ten thousand as themselves'. The sweet message of course echoes a long-standing trope articulated over the centuries among others by no less than William Shakespeare. In *As You Like It*, Act II, Scene VII, Jaques says to Duke Senior, 'All the world's a stage and all the men and women merely players.' The concept of life as an illusion that we participate in through play goes back to Platonism and Hinduism and yet has perhaps never been more materially relevant than today's age of 'reality everything'.

Much can be learned from the worlds of television, theatre and gameplay that is relevant to unlocking Collaborative Advantage. We'll explore how many of the conventions of gameplay can be harnessed to create Collaborative Advantage in the next chapter, but for now let's explore the contribution that can be made by adopting the concept of the format that defines the essence of the experience on offer in a distinct formula that can enable it to be extended and replicated in different territories as has been achieved with such television shows as *The Voice*, *Big Brother* and *Pop Idol*. All have been worldwide hits, albeit with different presenters and production teams. What most attracts you to your favourite shows or entertainment? What can you learn from that to help you shape the experiences you make available, directly or indirectly, to your own customers?

Play can be one of our most creative processes. Stuart Brown, co-author of the book *Play*,* argues that the opposite of 'play' is more realistically something akin to 'idleness' than 'work'. He argues that play, both in humans and in the animal kingdom, is vital to the process of adaptation, change and evolution. He suggests play acts as 'fertiliser for brain growth' and may have played a sufficient role in our evolution as a species for us to merit the classification '*Homo ludens*'.

Brown usefully identifies eight play archetypes that I would suggest could be used to identify opportunities to convert user experiences into 'formats' of play. These are comprised of:

- The **joker** who loves being the class clown and delights in nonsensical play.

- The **kinesthete** who needs to move and physically play, just for the sake of moving.

---

* Stuart Brown MD and Christopher Vaughan, *Play* (New York: Penguin, 2010), 65–70.

- The **explorer** who loves to indulge in new experiences, whether physical, mental, emotional or relational.

- The **competitor** who thrives on winning and being the best.

- The **director** who loves organising and directing the flow of play in groups.

- The **collector** who loves to curate their collections, whether experiential or material.

- The **artist**, or **creator**, who finds joy in making things.

- And the **storyteller** who is interested in unlocking stories and tapping into imagination.

These archetypes can each be associated with useful opportunities to engage your customers and others in activities that add value to your business. This could be through powerful consumer storytelling, driving loyalty, supporting customers in bringing their peers together, allowing your best customers to identify themselves, working with your most curious customers as pioneers of your future, giving your fans something to roll their sleeves up and do or simply relaxing and sharing some fun together.

Breathing fire

Greg Glassman, the founder of CrossFit, could certainly claim to know something about identifying formats and inviting participation in intense (-ly rewarding?) forms of play. CrossFit has been promoted as a philosophy of exercise and a competitive sport and has amassed a global social movement.

The core insight on which CrossFit is based is the observation that no single sport provides a measure of our overall fitness. While most sports require and develop a high level of fitness, much of that fitness is very specific to the sport in question. Having played tennis extensively growing up I know first-hand, for example, that tennis can result in making players much more physically developed on the side of their playing arm: not a particular boon to overall fitness! In fact, I remember my coach at the time having worried his doctor who at first believed he might have contracted a disease which attacked the muscles down the left side of his body, such was the difference in development between his left and right arms.

The core CrossFit proposition is to participate in demanding workouts consisting of a variety of aerobic, bodyweight and Olympic weightlifting challenges that are often timed and scored to promote competitive performance and individual progress and which are designed to build overall strength and conditioning across a broad range of parameters. Think of it as turning fitness itself into a sport. Or more specifically, as Glassman indicates, CrossFit is designed to build cardiovascular and respiratory endurance, stamina, strength, flexibility, power, speed, coordination, agility, balance and accuracy. It prides itself on being at the extreme end of fitness. Glassman knew he'd identified a special new way of working out when he could barely stop himself from throwing up after his early workouts.

Having created the sport, Glassman and CrossFit, Inc. developed a compelling set of unique formats for participating in it. CrossFit can now be learned and practised in over thirteen thousand gyms in the USA and around the world that are affiliated rather than owned by CrossFit, Inc., and that are known as 'Boxes'. CrossFit, Inc. earns revenue from annual licence fees and from certification programmes for the trainers.

At each Box you can participate in a 'Workout of the Day' or 'WOD', each with its own name, most commonly a female name (many of the workouts have been dubbed 'nasty girls' because they can have such a debilitating effect in the moment'). CrossFit practitioners have also developed the custom of referring to each other as 'fire breathers' to reflect the intensity of the efforts to which they are willing to commit. Adapted formats have also been made available, such as CrossFit for children and for people interested in self-defence or who belong to specific groups such as the police or fire services.

And since 2007 CrossFit has held its own CrossFit Games, a global competition with regional heats with the ambition to identify the world's fittest men and women. The games include formats that are not revealed to the athletes until hours before the competition, demanding them to be ready for any kind of challenge.

CrossFit is not without its critics. Some have argued that the sport can cause unnecessary injuries and others dislike its approach to social media that can include controversial claims about topics that reach beyond CrossFit itself. But the tough social fitness format appealed to sportswear manufacturer Reebok, which became a long-standing sponsor of the CrossFit Games and used the sport as the basis for developing lines of specialised clothing for more extreme fitness practitioners.

Quick review

- Step Two of Outside In enables external participation by identifying useful and engaging ways for people to participate.

- Traditional forms of marketing can often be replaced by providing more useful opportunities for customers to use products and services.

* For an account of the development of CrossFit read J. C. Herz, *Learning to Breathe Fire: The Rise of CrossFit and the Primal Future of Fitness* (New York: Three Rivers Press, 2014).

- This Step asks us to think less about what we supply and more about how people use what we supply and how we can make that usage more effortless, enjoyable or productive.

- This can involve re-imagining the user experience and drawing on models of play and participation that identify new opportunities for participation that can open the door to greater business value.

- It can be used to build an innovation pipeline for a business that channels the creation of Collaborative Advantage through myriad forms of valuable customer participation.

- These can often also form the basis for reaching new categories of customer and for creating new partnerships.

Step Two: strategic audit

1 How do your stakeholders currently experience your products, services or programmes? What are they really trying to do? What obstacles do they face and how might these be overcome?

2 What benefits can be created for your customers or beneficiaries by better supporting them in using your products, services and programmes?

3 What new experiences can you offer to enable participation? If these activities were a sport or a game, what would they be called and why?

4 How could these activities be divided into constituent parts? Or how might they be extended into a series?

5 What is the right business model for these activities? Should customers be asked to pay for them directly as a new source of revenue? If so, how (Individual payments? A subscription?)?

6 What other benefits can they create for your organisation as an alternative to conventional forms of marketing?

CHAPTER EIGHT

Step Three: engage participation

OUTSIDE IN

Step Three is about creating an environment conducive to the kind of pursuit that you have defined in Step One and enabled in Step Two.

This is about defining the rules of the game; creating different roles, for example, for different stakeholder groups or for people with differing levels of interest and commitment to play and creating the social customs, habits and rituals that support people participating alongside each other in your offerings.

This can represent one of the most powerful ways there are for influencing people you are not in charge of. When you define the rules of the game, you have a substantial influence over anyone who chooses to play it. I often wonder if the people who first codified the rules of soccer, for example, had any idea of the number of people whose behaviour they would influence as a result. Whether the activities and experiences you choose to enable in the pursuit of your brand agenda are literally games or different types of experience, setting the boundary conditions of participation can make the difference between success and failure.

What the world learned from eBay

Some of the most successful peer-to-peer platforms were created by founders and management teams who didn't necessarily initially invest that much in developing their brand image. What many did make sure to get right from the start, however, was to create an environment of protocols that truly supported peer-to-peer interaction. In the words of one commentator, eBay for example, 'taught millions of strangers to trust one another'.* It's arguable that eBay's understanding of human behaviour has been more crucial to its success than its understanding of technology. Its founder has said that the eBay 'brand experience is based on how one customer treats another

---

* Elen Lewis, *The eBay Phenomenon: How One Brand Taught Millions of Strangers to Trust One Another* (London: Marshall Cavendish, 2008).

customer'.* When they still had only thirty members of staff they were already defining the behaviour of over half a million users in terms of how they dealt with their used and unwanted but usually still functional possessions.

And when they faced early competition backed by much larger and more powerful organisations, they overcame the challenge not because of traditional competitive strengths but rather due to the loyalty of their users – or perhaps more precisely the loyalty their users had developed to each other through their feedback mechanisms. People did not want to switch to another platform and lose their user and seller ratings.

Who would you give your car keys to?

Trust and feedback mechanisms have become a key foundation of many collaborative business models. easyCar Club is a peer-to-peer car rental service that greatly depends on enabling people to trust one another. Believing someone will lend you a safe car or allowing someone to drive what may likely be your second-most valuable asset after your home, both require a high level of trust. This is something easy-Car cannot leave to chance.

So easyCar Club performs database checks in advance to make sure that people are who they say they are, have a decent driving record and don't have too many insurance claims. They also use video call technology, requiring all of the renters who sign up to show them the licence to make sure that the person who's applying matches the face on the driving licence.

---

* Donna L. Hoffman and Thomas P. Novak, *Beyond the Basics: Research-Based Rules for Internet Retailing Advantage* (Nashville: Vanderbilt University eLab Press, 2005).

And then once people are part of the Club, easyCar works to ensure that people follow the rules and act in a decent way, for example in the way they handle damage reports. And they have developed their own peer review mechanism to further encourage good participation.

But easyCar is not content with these protocols alone, as Richard Laughton, chief executive, explains: 'As they say in the fund management industry, past performance is no guarantee of future results so there is this concern still, I think, that no matter how well someone has been vetted in the past you still don't know how someone's going to drive your car when they pick up the keys. And so that is another piece of the trust angle that we're dealing with through technology.'*

It's early days at the moment but easyCar Club is already experimenting with a range of technologies to further increase user trust. As Richard explains, 'We've been talking for a long time about the "Internet of Things". But we're now seeing more and more sensors installed – not only in cars obviously, but in houses and elsewhere, and these feed back bits of information which we can use either to monitor in real time or to monitor after the event how things have been used. In particular, in the case of cars, you've got telematics which tracks where a car is going and how it's being driven; onboard diagnostics which will tell you whether there's a pre-existing problem with the engine, whether something arises during the course of a rental and, of course, things like dash cams, which mean that if you are involved in an accident or if there is a collision, you've got a much better view of how it was caused, who's at fault and therefore how that gets settled.'

* Richard's comments were made at the Westminster eForum on the Sharing Economy in the UK.

Building trust between users enables a network to collaborate effectively and feedback mechanisms provide signals that enable people to make better choices and increase their performance and satisfaction over time.

What's yours?

Countless sites and apps have drawn inspiration from these kinds of approach in what has become called the 'collaborative economy' to provide platforms for everything from currency exchange between holidays, to freelancing, to taking on chores for cash. A useful exercise when you are building participatory initiatives is to go back to sites such as these; to identify the ways in which they break down user interactions; and to pick out what your own equivalents might be.

I once ran a workshop for a group of humanitarian agencies in which we took this approach. They picked out the 'Watch this item' function on eBay, realising that there was no central platform for identifying and monitoring looming humanitarian crises, even though in responding to humanitarian disasters the need for that kind of tool is readily apparent.

Interestingly, two months after our workshop Google launched such a platform under the name of 'Public Alerts' for individuals who may know people affected by a disaster. A number of specialist agencies have also since been formed to offer a similar service but designed for the needs of humanitarian practitioners. I have since learned that the website that first housed eBay was also a portal for a website providing updates on Ebola outbreaks. So eBay's founder, Pierre Omidyar, may well have approved of the insights generated by the workshop.

Roles, customs and rituals

Other possibilities can be opened up by giving your customers a greater role in the creation and promotion of your products, programmes and services. Walkers, the snack food manufacturer, did exactly that when they set aside their own internal new product development programme and invited the public to invent and market six new flavours of crisps in three months with their 'Do us a flavour' campaign, which drove an 8.4 per cent increase in value sales of the brand. Walkers decided to repeat the initiative six years later, which led to a forty-year-old dad from Westcliff-on-Sea, Essex, winning the competition with his proposed flavour of pulled pork in a sticky BBQ sauce. He also pocketed a tasty cheque for one million pounds from Walkers for his contribution.

Just as in Step Two we explored the ways in which different play archetypes could be used to identify game-inspired formats for participation, when thinking about socialising the process to enable participation among peers we can also turn to the world of game typologies to identify roles for people to play within the game.

The Bartle taxonomy of player types is a classification of videogame players based on a paper by Richard Bartle,* but why not use it as a source of inspiration for designing participation in the use of your products and services? Are your users 'killers', who are interested in doing something to each other; 'achievers', interested in doing something to the game; 'socialisers', interested in doing something with others or 'explorers', interested in discovering something new? These typologies can be explored as you set what game developers refer to as your 'win condition' and identify your feedback mechanisms to give your challenge the epic feel of a legendary contest.

* Richard Bartle, 'Hearts, Clubs, Diamonds, Spades: Players Who Suit MUDS [Multi-User Dungeons]', (1996) https://mud.co.uk/richard/heds.htm.

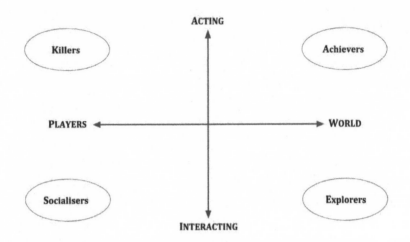

R. Bartle's typology of gaming preferences.

....

What possibilities could you open up by giving your customers a greater role in the creation or delivery of your core offering?

....

Building on people's existing habits can also be an effective way to unlock engagement. When P&G's air freshener, Febreze, was launched it wasn't initially a great success. The consumer insight team identified that people already believe their homes to be clean and did not feel the air freshener was necessary. So P&G turned to a parallel activity of washing clothes and identified the habit many people have of smelling their clothes when they take them out of the tumble drier after washing. P&G then re-positioned Febreze as something you use after you've cleaned the house to be able to appreciate that same freshness, thereby extending our existing habit from one domain of cleaning by translating it into another.

Instigating new rituals that people can return to over time is a powerful technique for unlocking repeat usage or socialised participation. Think of the way Google punctuates the calendar with its Doodles that mark special days of interest by adding a playful and interactive visual interest to its minimalist homepage. Or the way the mobile network Orange, now known as EE, created Orange Wednesdays to encourage people along to the cinema with their friends as a repeated action with a better deal. Or the way the WWF created Earth Hour as an annual opportunity to do one thing for the environment and take stock of where we stand on climate change and resource depletion.

Sleight of brand

Our choices are substantially influenced by the context in which they are made. The very act of cognition is understood by some psychologists almost as if it takes place outside the body, such is the degree to which our environment influences and shapes our thoughts (see also footnote on page 203). The creative application of insights from the field of behavioural economics has the potential to make a significant contribution to designing environments that are conducive to active participation and collaboration.

Juliet Hodges is a behavioural economist currently working as a behaviour change adviser at Bupa. I met Juliet through her involvement in supporting a number of charities with pro bono behaviour change services through the social enterprise I founded, Pimp My Cause. Juliet explains that behavioural economics is the lovechild of economics and psychology, drawing on decades of research in cognitive, social and evolutionary psychology to provide a better understanding of consumer behaviour. This approach is particularly useful in unlocking Collaborative Advantage because it helps us develop targeted, low-cost solutions based on the specific drivers and barriers to behaviour, which can maximise the likelihood of their active participation.

Juliet suggests five principles that can be creatively applied to enhance the Collaborative Advantage that you can build.

1. Make it easy

Humans are incredible. We built the Sistine Chapel, discovered electricity, travelled to the moon and invented the internet. But we can also be really quite lazy. The more complicated an action is, the less likely we are to do it. Removing friction in a process, even just an extra click of a button, can be more motivating for people than added incentives.

The government's Behavioural Insights Team discovered this in an effort to encourage more people to have loft insulation installed.[*] Although there are clear benefits, both environmentally and financially, for having a well-insulated home, it's still a hard sell. In this trial, people were offered cost-price loft insulation or a more expensive version including a loft-clearing service. People were much more likely to spend the extra money to have their attic cleared as well as insulated. Presumably, the barrier of having to clean out one's own attic was enough to make the cheap insulation unappealing.

Another example of this is choice paralysis. When there are too many options, we feel overwhelmed and don't choose anything at all. This is sometimes trivial – when there are too many flavours of jam at the supermarket, we're less likely to buy.[†] But we're also rubbish at deciding even when not doing so can have drastic consequences, like pension plans. As the number of different fund options increases, the likelihood of enrolling decreases.[‡]

---

[*] Department of Energy and Climate Change, 'Removing the Hassle Factor Associated With Loft Insulation: Results Of A Behavioural Trial', 2013, www.gov.uk/government/uploads/system/uploads/attachment_data/file/236858/DECC_loft_clearance_trial_report_final.pdf

[†] Iyengar & Lepper, 'When Choice is Demotivating: Can One Desire Too Much of a Good Thing?', 2000, faculty.washington.edu/jdb/345/345%20Articles/Iyengar%20%26%20Lepper%20(2000).pdf

[‡] Sheena S. Iyengar, Wei Jiang and Gur Huberman, 'How Much Choice is Too Much?: Contributions to 401(k) Retirement Plans', 2003, www.nagdca.org/dnn/Portals/45/2015Annual/16.%20How%20much%20choice%20is%20too%20much%20choice.pdf

Some brands know this instinctively. Apple, for example, may dominate the smartphone market partly because there are only a limited number of iPhone models. People tend to just go with the flow, so creating a default setting or auto-enrolment process can greatly increase adoption. This is something else Apple have harnessed. When Apple Pay first launched, cards had to be entered manually, with the result that only true enthusiasts used it initially. Later versions, however, required adding the necessary information when setting up a new phone. Opting people into it in this way helped it to become much more commonplace, with the majority of stores in the UK removing the upper limit on how much can be spent using Apple Pay.*

2. Create commitment opportunities

Humans tend to struggle with planning ahead. That's not really our fault, Juliet explains, because when early humans first appeared on the scene, they were more worried about consuming enough calories on a daily basis than planning their post-retirement finances decades in advance. In fact, when we think about our future selves, it activates the same part of the brain that we use to think about other people.† In other words, when we put something off until tomorrow, it feels like someone else will have to do it. It also means that we respond better to rewards right now than rewards in the future.

There is one way to overcome this present–future empathy gap: making a commitment ahead of time. Once we've said we'll do

---

* James Titcomb, 'Tipping point for Apple Pay as majority of UK tills accept limitless payments', *Daily Telegraph*, 21 May 2017, www.telegraph.co.uk/technology/2017/05/21/tipping-point-apple-pay-majority-uk-tills-accept-limitless-payments/
† Hal Ersner-Hershfield, G. Elliott Wimmer and Brian Knutson, 'Saving for the Future Self: Neural Measures of Future Self-Continuity Predict Temporal Discounting', *Social Cognitive and Affective Neuroscience*, March 2009, Vol. 4, Issue 1, 85–92, www.ncbi.nlm.nih.gov/pmc/articles/PMC2656877

something, whether publicly or privately, we become more likely to do so. In one study, participants were phoned ahead of an election and asked if they were intending to vote. Just telling a stranger on the phone they were going to vote meant they were much more likely to.[*] Making public commitments, such as a social media post, are even more powerful.

Interestingly, a small commitment can change our self-perception and influence our behaviour in the future. This is known as the 'foot in the door' effect.[†] It has been suggested that high-end shops give their customers champagne not to quench their thirst, but to create a perception of themselves as consumers of luxury items. This makes them more likely to continue investing in this perception by buying designer goods.

3. Put some skin in the game

We respond much more viscerally to the threat of losses than we do to the opportunity of reward. This effect is called 'loss aversion'. Losses, Juliet argues, feel around twice as painful to us as gains feel good.[‡] Any time you book a hotel, you'll see techniques that take advantage of this bias. Banners letting you know that 'Nineteen people are viewing this room right now!', 'Six rooms booked today!' or 'One room left!' are specifically designed to make you worry about missing out, a notion

* David W. Nickerson and Todd Rogers, 'Do You Have a Voting Plan? Implementation Intentions, Voter Turnout and Organic Plan Making', *Psychological Science*, 2010, Vol. 21, 194, scholar.harvard.edu/files/todd_rogers/files/do_you_have_a_voting_plan_0.pdf

† Jonathan L. Freedman and Scott C. Fraser, 'Compliance Without Pressure: the Foot-in-the-Door Technique', *Journal of Personality and Social Psychology*, 1966, vol. 4, no. 2, 155–202, psycnet.apa.org/record/1966-10825-001

‡ Daniel Kahneman, Jack L. Knetsch, Richard H. Thaler, 'Anomalies: the Endowment Effect, Loss Aversion and Status Quo Bias', *The Journal of Economic Perspectives*, winter 1991, Vol. 5, No. 1, 193–206, www.princeton.edu/~kahneman/docs/Publications/Anomalies_DK_JLK_RHT_1991.pdf

that has now been popularised by the phrase 'FoMO' or 'Fear of Missing Out'. These scare tactics are often more likely to result in you booking a room than you would had you read a list of its positive attributes.

This effect can be increased by inducing a sense of ownership. Juliet refers to a study in a university in which half of the students entering the lecture theatre were given a free mug.[*] They were then asked how much they would sell their mug for, while the students who hadn't been given a mug were asked how much they would pay to buy one. The mug owners wanted more than double the amount the others were willing to pay, which shows how even the briefest ownership can bias our perception of value.

Adding a dimension of personalisation can also be a great way to give people a sense of ownership as well as to grab their attention in the first place. This further explains the success of the 'Share a Coke' campaign mentioned previously, with names printed on Coca-Cola bottles. Very few people will see a Coke bottle with their name on it without feeling a desire to purchase it. The campaign was hugely successful, with a two per cent increase in sales across the USA.[†]

4. Choose the right messenger

The person or group of people communicating the information is often as important as the information you want to convey. Juliet cites the example of toothpaste commercials. When advertising its whitening and cosmetic properties, you're more likely to see a model or celebrity; when the advert is talking about enamel or reducing plaque, it's more likely to be a dentist in a white coat. We take in information differently from different sources.

[*] 'Compliance without pressure', op. cit.
[†] Mike Esterl, '"Share a Coke" Credited With a Pop in Sales', *Wall Street Journal*, 25 September 2014, www.wsj.com/articles/share-a-coke-credited-with-a-pop-in-sales-1411661519

Social norms are also reliable influencers of behaviour. We're herd animals and like to do what others around us are doing; the more similar they are to us, the better. A classic study of this phenomenon looked at rates of towel reuse in hotels. When guests were told that the majority of guests reused their towels, they were more likely to reuse their own than the control study who were given a pro-environment rationale for reuse.* In fact, when guests were told the majority of guests who had previously stayed in their room reused their towels, reuse rates increased even further.

However, there can also be unintended consequences for using the wrong norm or messenger. Opower, an energy provider in the States, showed their customers what their neighbourhood norm for energy use was and how their usage compared.† Those who were using less than average actually increased their use as a result of being given this information. That is, until Opower started including a smiley face on their bills, positively reinforcing their low usage by interpreting it as a superior performance.

5. Don't trust anybody
The prevailing theory in behavioural economics is that the vast majority of our decisions are made unconsciously. We don't analyse the pros and cons of every purchase, meal or action and our decisions are instead shaped by forces we may not even be aware of. This doesn't necessarily make us 'irrational' (as is often suggested), but our decisions are often suited to the context we're operating in and this behaviour helps us respond to information more quickly.

* Noah J. Goldstein, Robert B. Cialdini and Vladas Griskevicius, 'A Room with a Viewpoint: Using Social Norms to Motivate Environmental Conservation in Hotels', *Journal of Consumer Research*, October 2008, vol. 35, no. 3, 472–82, www.jstor.org/stable/10.1086/586910
† Hunt Allcott, 'Social Norms and Energy Conservation', *Journal of Public Economics*, October 2011, vol. 95, issues 9–10, 1082–1095, www.sciencedirect.com/science/article/pii/S0047272711000478

However, it does often mean we have no idea what we're talking about when we start trying to explain those choices. One study offered participants a choice of two photographs, and asked them to choose which person they found more attractive.[*] The photos were then surreptitiously swapped, so the participant was shown the person they didn't choose and asked to give reasons for their choice. Almost none of the participants picked up on the switch and happily elaborated on their decision with no idea they hadn't selected this person at all. More surprisingly still, they even gave reasons that couldn't possibly have been true. Some said they had chosen the brunette because that was their preferred hair colour, when they had actually chosen the blonde.

This lack of introspective access was also demonstrated by the energy example we looked at earlier. In a very similar study, people were asked which message they thought would be the most successful in changing their behaviour: the social norm, the money saved or the environmental plea. The social norm was rated as the least likely to be effective, when it was actually the most.[†]

What this means, unhelpfully, is that it's often pointless as a market research exercise to simply ask people what they want. Juliet explains how banks may have found this out the hard way when trying to increase use of their online services. Customers have indicated that security concerns are the main reason they hadn't adopted this new technology, but investing heavily in added security doesn't

---

[*] Petter Johansson, Lars Hall, Sverker Sikström and Andreas Olsson, 'Failure to Detect Mismatches Between Intention and Outcome in a Simple Decision Task', *Science*, 7 October 2005, Vol. 310, Issue 5745, 116–119, people. hss.caltech.edu/~camerer/NYU/olson.pdf

[†] Jessica M. Nolan, P. Wesley Schultz, Robert B. Cialdini, Noah J. Goldstein and Vladas Griskevicius, 'Normative Social Influence is Under-detected', *Personality and Social Psychology Bulletin*, 2008, Vol. 34, 913, citeseerx.ist. psu.edu/viewdoc/download?doi=10.1.1.431.5682&rep=rep1&type=pdf

necessarily improve adoption rates. Some suggest that most people just don't understand this new technology, so banks would be better off investing in computer literacy than security measures.

Quick review

- Step Three of Outside In is about creating an environment conducive to participation in the use of your products and service offerings.

- It can be thought of as framing the rules of a game and can be a powerful way to influence customer and other stakeholder behaviour.

- It may involve defining roles for different people to play according to their varying levels of interest and capability.

- It may also involve creating or working with established social norms, customs, habits and rituals that can support people in participating alongside each other.

- This step also helps you apply the glue of trust between customers and you and, where needed, between users and each other.

- The latest insights from the behavioural sciences show the benefits in making it easy for people to join in, commit to participating and listening to your advocates.

Step Three: strategic audit

1 How can you create the right environment for customer and stakeholder participation?

2 What are the 'rules of the game' for the activities you seek to enable? How can you make these fair, useful and appealing?

3 What roles can be designed for different customer or stakeholder groups to play?

4 How can you enable participants to trust and participate alongside each other in pursuing this interest?

5 What habits do your desired participants already have that may be of relevance? How can these habits be used to unlock their participation?

6 What new habits, rituals or social norms can you create to embed their participation more strongly? How can this be achieved in a way that works with people's true decision-making processes?

CHAPTER NINE

Step Four: iterate and accelerate

OUTSIDE IN

STEP 4 **ITERATE AND ACCELERATE**
STEP 3 **ENGAGE PARTICIPATION**
STEP 2 **CREATE OPPORTUNITIES**
STEP 1 **FIND COMMON PURPOSE**

Step Four consists of developing a deeper understanding of your early adopters in order to be able to better address their needs and to use their influence to reach a broader mainstream.

This step often involves looking closely at the challenges faced by users and identifying ways to overcome them so that participation can scale from the willing few to the many who will join them if it's easy enough to do so.

Andrew Chapin, formerly of Uber's driver operations group, for example, reflected on the fact that more drivers meant more available rides which led to more passengers which in turn meant more fares which encouraged more drivers. He realised that the positive cycle of drivers and passengers could be further accelerated if more passengers had the financial means to buy cars that they could use to become Uber drivers themselves. So he introduced a financing mechanism whereby Uber could act as an intermediary between finance companies and would-be Uber drivers, guaranteeing car loans and enabling repayments to be sent directly to the lenders from the Uber fares earned.

This step of Outside In can also be about actively enabling your early adopters themselves to make a bigger contribution to the process of innovation. Picking up on our previous example of eBay, much of their most interesting and useful innovation has come from its users. Even the first 'sniper' software – enabling buyers to outbid each other at the last second – was written by a community member.

This step can also be achieved by getting the details right, enabling the most enjoyable and frictionless participation possible. This is done through the accumulation of small changes, based on watching carefully how people participate and taking measures to improve each aspect of their experience.

As one illustration, a number of peer-to-peer websites have noticed that five-star user ratings have become, counter-intuitively, rather binary. People tend to give five stars without thinking about it if they are happy, and fewer stars tends to mean not that they were relatively satisfied but that they were distinctly dissatisfied. So an increasing number of such sites are experimenting with a seven-star system. The insight seems to be that when presented with the option of adding the extra two stars, people tend to dwell on the decision for a moment longer and give more thoughtful and differentiating reviews.

In a similar instance, car-pooling platform BlaBlaCar has taken a different approach to differentiating self-ratings. The ride-sharing site asks members to rate themselves according to what they believe to be the key variable we should use when deciding who to go on a long journey with: how much they like to talk. People can rate themselves as 'Bla' if they are fairly quiet, 'Bla, bla' if they are moderate talkers and 'Bla, bla, bla' if they like to gabble on through the whole journey!

Bridging the divide

Working with early adopters to understand their needs and use their influence to achieve scale makes this step of Outside In useful in addressing what is statistically one of the most common problems for new business offerings. Businesses often manage successfully to generate early sales but struggle thereafter to scale their sales sufficiently to sustain their activities over time. Addressing this kind of challenge has often been referred to as 'crossing the chasm', after Geoffrey Moore's book on the subject.[*]

By revealing and addressing a more sophisticated understanding of needs, this step can also be used to build longevity in what may

---

[*] Geoffrey A. Moore, *Crossing the Chasm: Marketing and Selling Disruptive Products to Mainstream Customers* (New York: HarperCollins, 1991).

otherwise be 'Here this morning, gone by this evening' environments typical of markets that are traditionally dominated by price point promotions.

. . . .

Look closely at the challenges faced by users and identify ways to overcome them so that participation can scale from the willing few to the many who will join them if only you can make it easy enough.

. . . .

Show me the money

Working with early adopters does not just mean asking them what they want and giving it to them. Economists use the term 'revealed preference'* to describe patterns of consumer demand that can be understood through purchasing behaviour in practice rather than stated preference.

Quirky.com is a platform that crowd-sourced ideas for new product inventions and then engaged its members in designing and developing those inventions. What I loved about Quirky was a concept they developed early on called 'threshold': they pre-sold their products to their members when they reached the prototype stage, but they didn't actually commit to manufacturing until a sufficient number of members had pre-purchased the product for them to know they would be likely to return a profit. That also gave them the chance to approach mainstream retailers offering them the proposition to carry a product that had never previously been available but for which there was already substantial evidence of its likely commercial success.

* 'Revealed preference' theory was originally developed by American economist Paul Samuelson.

Quirky acquired over a million members and brought four hundred products to the shops. But selecting new products by online votes rather than continuing to ask people to commit their money to intended purchases diminished the ability of the crowd to correctly predict winners and left Quirky with too many expensive innovations that did not all succeed commercially. Participation alone does not necessarily build Collaborative Advantage; it must be built with a sound strategy that drives true value creation.

Learning from early adopters

Even when users are not contributing to the innovation process directly, there is of course so much we can learn from them to help us grow our business. I doubt that easyCar Club, the car peer-to-peer rental platform we looked at earlier, could have predicted in advance that eighty per cent of its rentals would take place at weekends. But discovering that to be the case when observing early adopters opened the door to actions that actively work to support that trend. So easy-Car decided to invest in developing and advertising additional services that support people in enjoying short breaks away from the city at the end of the working week.

Elsewhere we find Grub Club, the online club we looked at earlier that provides unique one-off dining experiences by matching chefs, diners and unusual venues that can be turned into a kitchen often for one night only. They provide another example of learning from early adopters. In market testing, chefs had been rather sceptical about the concept while diners had loved the idea. So the founders believed that they should focus their marketing efforts on convincing chefs to participate. But once the site was up and running, it was quickly learned that contrary to the preliminary indications, chefs were in fact extremely willing to join, and that the real challenge was recruiting diners and motivating them to take action rather than just find the idea intriguing.

In 2004, Lego was close to bankruptcy. But with a new CEO came a mandate for a new direction. Lego identified adults who had grown up with Lego as a latent reservoir of energy, ideas and influence. They began working with these super fans to develop new ideas for kits and ultimately created their Lego Ideas portal specifically to open up and catalyse the process. Once they identified usable ideas they then started to accelerate the design process by prototyping new kits with just a few key features and working with their supporters to complete their specification. This approach has made a key contribution to re-establishing Lego as one of the most powerful brands in the world.

Bring a friend

Using peer influence can also be seen in the way global brands adapt their offering to particular countries, enabling early adopters of their core proposition to bring with them people who prefer to stay with their own customs. Such an instance can be seen when McDonald's offers a shot of espresso and three mini-pastries as Le Café Gourmand in its French restaurants or when Starbucks offers a special line of teas in China including MuDan white tea, Jinxuan Oolong and Biluochun green tea. A similar principle lies more explicitly behind Domino's campaign promoting their salads. Domino's Pizza is unlikely to ever become the mecca of salad lovers, but by providing salad options they avoid the risk of situations in which groups of people want to get pizza but the lack of salad as an option causes a health-conscious member of the group to veto the plan. In the words of their US commercial, the availability of their salad option prevents a family from having to miss out on pizza night for the sake of the salad-loving 'Dinner Dictator'.

This step in implementing the Outside In framework is supported by social research that shows crowd behaviour can best be thought of not as a matter of aggregating individual responses to a situation but rather as a product of patterns of peer-to-peer influence. By working to support the promoters of a new behaviour and giving them a greater influence over the group than that enjoyed by detractors, it's possible to catalyse phase transition changes in behaviour right across a social group. It works much in the same way that ice can be turned into water by warming the molecules at the bottom of the cube that pass the heat on through sequential layers.

A pertinent example can be seen in any nightclub on a Friday night. Early in the evening, most people are likely to be sitting down or standing at the bar rather than dancing. At a certain point a few people will get up or move across the floor to dance and rope their friends in until a critical point is reached and a sizeable portion of the people in the club have joined in. The number of people prepared to dance even if they are literally alone on the dance floor or who will not dance under any circumstances is relatively small. The actions of a few, however, can shift the majority from one mode to another. The draw is not just in the activity, but also in the other people pursuing that activity. This goes some way to explaining the success of marketing campaigns that involve their audience in the creative work of the campaign, working with their most enthusiastic customers to influence the rest.

The toy company Hasbro, for example, ran a campaign for Furby in which they partnered with Nickelodeon and Capital Radio on a campaign that saw different Furby characters competing for the prize of 'Furby Star'. Over three hundred thousand children voted for their favourite character as the storyline unfolded, influencing the creative development with their votes, reaching their friends by discussing the campaign online and downloading ringtones that supported the marketing of the toys at the end of the campaign.

The march of the copycats

Making the use of your product or service by your customers easy to spot – and copy – can also add tremendous value. Much may have been made in marketing literature about word-of-mouth marketing. Indeed, today's marketer also makes the distinction between classical word of mouth and online word of mouth (or eWOM). Online word of mouth includes online reviews, mechanisms for giving and sharing product and service feedback and conversation on social media. Marketers often seek to influence eWOM because it is visible to them in ways that offline conversation is not. People are no doubt sensible therefore to treat some of this content with a degree of scepticism, as it may be far less authentic and unbiased than it appears. But, in practice, the phenomenon of perceived usage can influence choices on a far greater scale than word-of-mouth recommendations.

When Canon painted the outside of their professional lenses white to protect them from intense sunlight, for example, they made it very easy for people to see photographers using Canon cameras at sporting events. Canon also systematically look for photos on the web that have been taken with their GoPro equipment and then promote them on their own platform to millions of viewers who can use the site to learn how to take great footage.

I'm convinced this also gets to the heart of the success of carbonated drinks. When you add bubbles to a Coke, you don't change the flavour. You don't make it more nutritious and you certainly don't make it easier to digest. But when you open the bottle the resulting 'pshhh' certainly lets everyone know you're about to enjoy a Coke. How many times have you sat working at your desk, deep in flow and unaware of any feeling of thirst until someone gets a Coke and suddenly you realise you could do with one too?

Bringing the data in sight

I would argue that data is not something that should be taken from users for no benefit in return. Nor are the insights that can be gleaned from an effective approach to data analysis and customer insight something that a business seeking to grow can ignore or fail to work with effectively. Understanding people in context is at the heart of making sense of data.

I'm a member of a council-run local gym and use a private gym on bank holidays when the council gym is closed. I would argue that the two gyms both get their approach to customer insight wrong, for very different reasons.

I love the council-run gym. It is not pretty. But it is massively functional. And while you'd think that a council-run gym might overdo it a bit on regulations and bureaucracy, mine is run by a team apparently unencumbered by the kind of systems that might prevent common-sense decision-making on the gym floor. 'New to the area? Come in and try the facilities with no paperwork or restrictions.' The only criticism I'd make is that by not actively learning everything they can from users, they may be leaving inspiration for great ideas on the table that could otherwise be adding value.

The branded gym, however, employs the opposite approach which, I'm afraid, can feel more like a customer-control system than a customer-service system. Many gyms offer free single-day access to interested users in exchange for key information concerning their preferences that they can use to drive their marketing and sales, in a viable act of collaboration for mutual benefit. But this particular gym requires pages and pages of data entry for the privilege of buying a single-day pass. They are so keen to capture the data that I've been told when the computers that are used to collect the data are down a day-pass can't be bought. In addition, I've filled in their digital forms a number of times and on each occasion requested no emails or texts, but I end up spammed with messages I don't want to receive. And, as for far more useful information that I have offered to staff in person rather than through their system, that seems to get ignored too. Now that's not anything resembling cooperation.

And it may further be self-defeating in that practices like these that may have contributed to the creation of an environment in which new regulation, including new European Union general data protection regulations, can emerge. Some believe this may ultimately pose an existential threat to many forms of direct marketing.

How can data insight be used ethically to learn from early adopters how best to reach a broader mainstream? How can it be used to unlock the most effective consumer participation in the propositions we bring to market?

Heather Wade is a former head of insight for eBay and dunnhumby and now works as a consultant, advising businesses on how to develop their data and customer insight strategy. I met Heather through her participation in my social enterprise, Pimp My Cause, and asked her to lift the veil on the opportunity that the availability of data and new analytical techniques can present for businesses of all sizes.

Heather argues that data and customer insight can best be understood as a foundation for collaboration 'driven by a genuine curiosity to better understand your customer and to identify ways to better meet their needs while adding value to your organisation in the process'. She introduces three key principles that can get anyone off to a good start in making customer data work for them and the people they serve.

1. Love your customers more than your idea!
'You may think you have invented the most amazing product ever. It's a new technology, the packaging is great and it's extremely easy to use.

So why won't it sell? Potentially, you have not fully understood the market you were going into. How well do you know what your customers actually need as opposed to what you want to sell to them?'

This is not just a problem with start-up companies – many large companies have responded to market conditions by releasing products that never made it to mass adoption. Microsoft's Zune was developed in response to Apple products, but failed due to technical problems discovered by consumers on usage. Heather cites the classic example of Clairol misreading consumer desire for 'back-to-nature' products by launching Touch of Yoghurt Shampoo in the 1970s. Customers, quite understandably, didn't really associate dairy with shampoo, and some even tried to eat the product.

Heather advises to pull back and work on a more objective level of understanding of customer needs, the market potential and how you need to market the product.

2. Learn what to learn (and from whom)

'The kind of customer that finds you almost before you even launch your product has a very different lesson to teach than the kind that only buys your product when it has virtually become the default option in its market,' Heather explains. 'Early adopters have a lot of knowledge to share and that knowledge can best be captured through qualitative research. Spend as much time getting to know them as you can, even on an individual basis. They can reward this attention by becoming your market analysts, your spokespeople and your new idea generators. Keep your friends close but keep your early adopters closer.'

Heather argues that when it comes to the more conservative mainstream that your early adopters ultimately help you to reach, your quantitative data becomes your most valuable tool, opening the door to ways of scaling the propositions they helped you identify and bring to market. 'Different sources of data also help you answer different questions. Your quantitative data is going to give you an excellent view of what is happening, but not of why it is happening. Your qualitative data gives you in-depth why for a very small sample.' Combining both approaches thoughtfully can help you build a market understanding that can take you from successful launch to high-value growth.

3. Make everyone a people-watcher

Heather concludes by explaining the importance of using the insights you get from your data to think about how you will make your company more focused on the customer overall. 'Many companies think that the customer is "owned" by the chief marketing officer and data is owned by the chief information officer but really everyone should take responsibility for the customer experience.' This involves spending significant time and effort on your own business – educating people on the insights from the data, recommending what could change as a result and showing reliable measurements.

There are simple ways to do this from setting up a monthly 'voice of the customer' session, run by marketing and insights teams, to including customer metrics in your monthly scorecard reporting. Heather advises, 'To really make this impactful, you should include customer metrics in your evaluation process, with part of your year-end appraisal based on how your team has contributed to customer satisfaction.'

Hacking for growth

Related to the opportunity to learn from, work with and build on the influence of your early adopters, are the techniques that have come to be known as 'growth hacking'. Growth hacking has the potential to build on the potential already unlocked in Step Two to bypass traditional marketing methods by creating ways to offer more utility to your customers as a better way to drive adoption. With growth hacking, it becomes possible to do more to turn your customers into your marketing team. Aaron Ginn, blogger and growth hacker for organisations such as Everlane, StumbleUpon and Mitt Romney's 2012 US presidential campaign, phrases it nicely: 'The end goal of every growth hacker is to build a self-perpetuating marketing machine that reaches millions by itself.'* This can be achieved through successive iterations of tracking, testing and enhancing. How do people respond to our offer? What happens if we change the proposition? What improvements can we make based on this observation?

Just as Heather reminds us to take a human-centric approach to understanding and unlocking insight from data, Damian Ryan, author of *Understanding Digital Marketing* and ambassador for digital marketing for Pimp My Cause also reassures us that ultimately, growth hacking is about understanding people even more than it is about evolving technology. 'Don't overlook the fact that your customers are people too – marketing isn't a bad thing and neither is asking questions and engaging with people on a genuine one-to-one basis.'

He advises us not to be put off by preconceptions based on language. 'The expression "growth hacking" has never sat well with me personally. It conjures up images of bearded subversives cracking code in some disused warehouse. It reeks of black-hat tactics rather than creating a perception of something that should be standard practice. The same rules apply to growth hacking as with any common-sense marketing activity.'

Damian advises us to prioritise understanding our audience and even identifying what our audience is in the first place. He urges us to 'find out what keeps them up at night, where they experience pain or what irks them (is it growth hackers?)'. He suggests that if you're any good

* www.aginnt.com

at growth hacking you'll realise that the more you focus on being in the 'problem recognition' business, the more potential for contributing to your customers' lives you will identify and the more growth you will achieve.

Quick review

- Step Four of Outside In supports you in enhancing your proposition by working with your early adopters and most enthusiastic supporters to reach a broader mainstream market.

- It provides some of the most important techniques for growing revenue from early trials and niche appeal to high-volume and high-value opportunities.

- It provides the opportunity to capture value from early adopters to improve your product, improve your communications, overcome customer challenges, deliver more value and capture a greater return.

- It works with the techniques of data insight and growth hacking to test, improve, iterate and enhance your products and services.

- It helps you to build a more customer-focused business and to convert your customers into your strongest marketing asset.

Step Four: strategic audit

1 What most surprises you about how your early adopters use your products and services?

2 What can you learn from this and how can you improve your proposition as a result?

3 What are the biggest obstacles to growth that you currently face as an organisation?

4 How could customers and other groups outside the organisation help you overcome these obstacles? And how can you enable them to do this?

5 How can you make people's use of your products and services, or participation in activities that you've enabled, more visible to others?

6 Who are your most enthusiastic participants? How can you work with them to better understand and meet their needs and develop a better proposition for later adopters as a result?

CHAPTER TEN

Step Five: build partnerships

OUTSIDE IN

STEP 5 **BUILD PARTNERSHIPS**
STEP 4 **ITERATE AND ACCELERATE**
STEP 3 **ENGAGE PARTICIPATION**
STEP 2 **CREATE OPPORTUNITIES**
STEP 1 **FIND COMMON PURPOSE**

Step Five involves identifying and working with partners who can help you to grow faster and further than you could alone.

Antoine de Saint Exupéry argued that the perfect partnerships are based not on looking at each other, but rather on looking in the same direction.* Developing a powerful brand agenda and an approach to the business that invites value-creating contributions from a broad network of customers and supporters who buy into that agenda can open the door to identifying and building valuable partnerships that provide benefits to all involved.

Unlike the previous four steps, this can be applied at different stages in the process. Indeed, some of the examples we'll look at were born as partnerships. But I've included it as the final Step of Outside In to emphasise the impact that it can have in enabling rapid growth by granting access to a broader pool of talent, resources and networks.

Pimp My Cause

The experience of running Pimp My Cause to support charities and social enterprises through access to top marketing talent has taught me that Collaborative Advantage can be harnessed to increase the achievements of any organisation, no matter how slender its resources.

With a conventional approach based on nothing but what I own, manage or control (little more than my own time and that of a few colleagues), I would essentially have been limited to doing a bit of pro bono marketing alongside my commercial consulting work. I might have been able to persuade a few colleagues to join me if the projects I chose were particularly exciting. But the proposition of 'Marketing a

---

* 'Love does not consist in gazing at each other, but in looking outward together in the same direction', Antoine de Saint Exupéry, *Wind, Sand and Stars* (New York: Reynal & Hitchcock, 1939).

better world' is something that both individual marketers across the profession and many of the organisations they work for, or are members of, can support in myriad ways. By assembling a team of volunteers and creating Pimp My Cause as a platform to support this pursuit, we've been able to leverage a level of external talent and resource that has enabled us to create an exponentially greater impact than anything any of us could have achieved alone. We have been joined by thousands of individual marketers using our online matching service to support good causes. And working with our marketers and learning from them has enabled us to find ways to partner up with leading professional organisations, agencies and brands.

Pimp My Cause works because it's not only good for our organisations but good for our marketers too. Marketers often have a keen sense of the aspects of marketing they'd like to get better at, become better known for, or move into. It turns out that finding experience-led opportunities to develop these specific capabilities is not easy to come by. Marketers have used our network of charities and social enterprises in need of marketing support to find just the right opportunities for themselves over the past five years. And this is an experience that can be greatly accelerated with the right coaching support.

This has opened the door to developing a proposition for marketing teams to partner with Pimp My Cause on Challenges in the form of bespoke learning and development programmes with a positive social impact built around the marketing capabilities each brand partner's team seeks to enhance. They support our activities and those of our charities and social enterprise members while delivering an additional triple-win for our brand partners:

• Enhancing their marketing capabilities

• Helping them deliver on their business priorities

• Fulfilling their social purpose

The teams work in small groups, each of which is presented with a live marketing brief for an inspiring good cause that they have chosen from a shortlist. They then receive bespoke coaching support and usually achieve more than they thought possible in less time than they would have imagined. Challenge partnerships are particularly useful when a brand is looking to change the way its team is working to achieve its business objectives.

This approach has the potential to transform marketing performance. Traditional training programmes can be too theoretical and narrow, creating change that has a short life back on the job. They don't deliver enough return on investment. The Challenge programmes that we've designed with our marketers, on the other hand, provide a proposition that involves real-world problems, in an innovative format with high impact for all participants. They can deliver more for the business, more for its marketing teams and unlock significant benefits for society through the support provided for the good causes in the process.

Mark Evans, the chief marketer of the Direct Line Group, has described our Challenges as giving marketing teams 'the gift of a seemingly impossible challenge'. This can serve to:

- Raise ambition

- Diversify experience

- Change perceptions

- Increase creativity

- Foster trust

- Build leadership

Each Challenge focuses on particular marketing capabilities. For example, we worked with the Nectar team at Aimia to create a

Challenge programme focused on marketing innovation. This was developed in 2015, at a time when Aimia was re-structuring how the Nectar card – the loyalty reward scheme run by companies such as Sainsbury's – operates and was seeking to build deeper innovation capabilities in its marketing team. By supporting Nectar's marketers in building stakeholder engagement plans to drive the loyal participation of their charity partners' own customers, donors, volunteers and other partners, the Challenge demonstrated the contribution that loyalty can make to organisational success. It built the talent, experience and capabilities of the marketers and supported the causes with opportunities to become more financially sustainable and provide more support to their beneficiaries.

We have also learned much of what we know about the creative application of scientific understanding of behaviour change from our partnership with the advertising agency Ogilvy, which has now entered its fifth year. The Ogilvy Change team within Ogilvy works on three of our causes per year in a 'living laboratory' that demonstrates how the creative application of insights from the behavioural sciences can create positive social outcomes by changing people's behaviour. Ogilvy uses Pimp My Cause briefs as part of a summer programme run to engage marketers from across the industry in enhancing their ability to drive behaviour change. Ogilvy's own team then works on the briefs to deliver a complete client solution.

This approach has also opened the doors to further similar partnerships. For example, the Institute of Practitioners in Advertising (IPA) is the leading organisation delivering continuing professional development and talent development opportunities for advertising agencies. Their elite residential programmes are primarily aimed at senior agency staff and planners with two to four years of board level experience. These programmes combine keynote speakers, live hothouse strategic and creative development in teams and expert coaching and evaluation. Through our partnership with the IPA, Pimp My Cause briefs are used for their residential training programmes. They provide an inspiring challenge for the marketers involved and the causes come away with excellent marketing and communications plans. We have also provided briefs that are used in some of the IPA's prestigious awards programmes to showcase and support creative talent.

Pimp My Cause also works with senior marketers through its Marketing for Change partnership with the Marketing Society. This includes two themed member events per year in special locations with high-profile speakers, a pledging process that enables senior marketers to adopt a cause for a three-month period before passing it to another member and regular articles and thought leadership contributions on the Marketing Society's website and their other publications.

The potential is vast. We believe there are no marketing capabilities that cannot be built or enhanced through structured opportunities to improve the world around us.

David and Goliath join forces

Elsewhere too, 'little-and-large' partnerships sometimes offer the most attractive paths to scale. BMW invested in the JustPark app that enables drivers to find, book, pay for and navigate to parking spaces including those made available by home and business owners. They integrated the app's functionality in the dashboard of the Mini Cooper with plans to roll it out across their entire range of cars. This opens up over one hundred thousand parking places in the UK to BMW drivers and enables them to use the car's in-built navigation system to find them.

We could also look at the way in which large hotel groups have been investing in and partnering with home-sharing sites, enabling the groups to benefit from the sites' financial success, advertise their rooms through the sites and provide support services such as room cleaning. Examples already include Wyndham's investment in Love Home Swap, Hyatt Hotels' investment in Onefinestay or the related investment of the InterContinental Hotels Group in Stay.com, which provides local citizen city guides.

· ·

Collaborative Advantage can often best be unlocked by partnerships among strange bedfellows, where competitive considerations do not arise and where a shared agenda can be fully embraced as a reciprocal benefit.

· ·

Strange bedfellows

Something that further differentiates the Collaborative Advantage approach from conventional competitive approaches is that in a traditional context, the 'strategic group' of analysis (see also page 24) consists of the organisations which most resemble your own and are deemed to offer the greatest competitive threat. In creating Collaborative Advantage, however, partnerships are often best formed among strange bedfellows, where competitive considerations do not arise and where a shared agenda can be fully embraced as a reciprocal benefit.

Just such a great partnership of strange bedfellows was seen in the collaboration between Paddy Power and the leading gay rights campaigning charity Stonewall to run the Rainbow Laces campaign. Realising there was not a single openly gay professional footballer in the UK, Paddy Power sent rainbow laces to every player in the country, asking them to wear the laces as a sign of support for their 'Right behind gay footballers' campaign. They received worldwide coverage, amplified the interest through their own communications and social media, got over fifty professional clubs involved, were covered through more than four hundred news stories and even had a motion passed in parliament. A result for Paddy Power, a result for Stonewall and a result for inclusiveness in sport.

Other examples of such strange bedfellows include easyJet's partnering with Formula One to learn from their pit stops how they can accelerate their 'turn time' (how long it takes for a plane to be readied for its next flight after landing), a key determinant of profitability. Or Unilever's bypassing of traditional advertising through their Foundry, which directly fosters partnerships with technology companies that can develop interesting alternatives to conventional marketing. Through the Foundry, small tech companies get to reach a much larger market with their solutions and Unilever get to up their game in terms of understanding and making the most of new technology. Successes have included 'intelligent' ice cream fridges in newsagents that can communicate special offers to the mobile phones of passersby on hot days.

Sometimes the nature of the participation can also enable specific innovative propositions. A social enterprise supported by Pimp My Cause called FoodCycle has a non-financial 'triple-donation' model. Supermarkets provide surplus food, businesses with kitchens that are not in constant use supply excess capacity and FoodCycle's volunteers offer their time to prepare and serve meals to people otherwise unable to afford them.

Marriages of convenience

Although forging partnerships with other organisations that more closely resemble our own can be hard because they may risk or be perceived to risk creating win–lose outcomes, there are still many instances in which collaboration among similar organisations can be useful in driving growth. Examples include groups of businesses that identify opportunities to create mutual benefit by addressing shared problems on a scale that can't be achieved alone. Consumer goods or food companies may work together to ensure an increased sustainable supply of raw ingredients through the shared development of solutions that none of them would be large enough to develop on their own at an affordable cost.

Marriages of convenience can also be forged in situations where businesses can only access certain opportunities by working together. This can occur for example in particular business-to-business environments in which collaboration is required to successfully play a part in the supply chain of a large commercial customer. In a manufacturing context this may mean working extensively with other suppliers to ensure mutual compatibility of components. Or in a service industry it may mean collaborating with other service providers to build an integrated solution. Examples include a client brand working with a host of specialist marketing and advertising agencies on an integrated campaign requiring contributions from all their specialist disciplines.

In these cases there will still usually be a clear differentiation between the partners, although there is greater risk of one partner bringing in another part of their business or expanding their activities to shut out the other partner. This would not be so much of a concern in a partnership of strange bedfellows.

When all of the Steps of Outside In are applied, partnerships among similar organisations can be developed to achieve inspiring goals. I have had the good fortune to advise a humanitarian initiative called the Start Network since it first emerged from a pilot project called the Consortium of British Humanitarian Agencies (CBHA). It emerged as an outcome of a series of conversations among the humanitarian directors of the major UK-based NGOs including Oxfam and Save the

Children and in response to a proposition from the Department for International Development (DFID). The government would provide a new source of pre-positioned funding if a group of agencies could work together to provide the fastest and most effective responses possible to each crisis addressed.

The hope was that the mechanism could be used to address many of the smaller humanitarian crises that don't make the media headlines. The rationale for pre-positioning the funds was to ensure that they would already be available when each crisis hit. So the CBHA created a peer review mechanism to enable fast, transparent, collective decision-making in the selection of crises to address and the identification of those to provide the response on the ground based on needs. The logic of addressing smaller crises was based on the hope of preventing them from becoming larger scale problems by addressing them more quickly. This was reinforced by the observation that too often such smaller crises can be overlooked by the international system.

We therefore framed the purpose of the initiative with the brand agenda 'Accelerating crisis response'. And the CBHA expanded to include a more global membership base with leading NGOs from around the world and was re-named the Start Network. After several years of expansion, we realised that 'Accelerating crisis response' could no longer contain the ambition we collectively felt, not just to speed up support for affected communities but also to deeply change the nature of that support and the process that is used to provide it.

We explored whether the real problem was that crisis response can be too slow or if it is often also provided by the wrong people in the wrong way, with many of the most relevant sources of anticipation, preparedness and response all too often overlooked by the international humanitarian system. Ultimately, these questions led us to re-define Start's purpose and to re-brand its major services.

The Start Network moves away from a system that can seem as if it has a hammer and is looking for nails to use them on and towards one that begins with the needs of people affected by a crisis and from there tries to identify the right response to those needs, wherever it may come from. It is about 'connecting people affected by crisis with the best possible solutions'.

Through the Start Fund it seeks to provide the right funding at the right time to enable the best solutions from across a much greater range of possible options than could ever be available to an individual agency acting alone.

It uses Start Engage to build the right capabilities in the right places to increase and enhance the range of options we have. Crises can hit anywhere. We therefore all need to be prepared which requires the development of a whole-of-society approach. Start Engage seeks to work with often-overlooked resources that are already in place where a crisis hits and support them in enhancing the solutions they can provide.

And Start Labs seeks to connect the right ideas with the right people to provide better solutions for people in crisis through shared thinking, prototyping and rapid experimentation, including partnerships with the private sector. For example, it can develop financial tools, such as parametric insurance to avoid or alleviate suffering. Payments are released when climatic conditions indicate a disaster may be imminent rather than waiting until disaster has struck, suffering has been caused and the overall expense of a solution is greater.

The Start Network has worked tirelessly to engage its members, new members, donors, private sector partners and other collaborators in sharing these aspirations. Recently, for example, it has partnered with the government of Estonia and a technology firm that specialises in deploying blockchain* solutions to trial a new method of coordinating decision-making and funding allocations in real time. My belief is that with a goal that is so clearly worth pursuing, the Start Network will continue to find the right people to share its journey.

. . . .

The process of applying Outside In can be repeated through successive iterations both to refine strategy and to complement it by applying a similar approach to fresh initiatives and campaigns to create additional business value.

. . . .

New beginnings

Step Five has brought us to the end of a complete cycle of Outside In. That does not mark the end of the process of building strategic Collaborative Advantage, however.

The process of applying Outside In can be repeated through successive iterations both to refine strategy and to complement it by applying a similar approach to fresh initiatives and campaigns that can create additional business value. In a complex world of constant change, we need never stop learning from our environment, getting better at what we do or creating Collaborative Advantage. The following chapters explore the range and extent of the contribution it can make to our own success and to the difference we can make to our customers and the world around us.

---

* A blockchain is a decentralised digital ledger that records transactions in such a way that they cannot be altered retrospectively. They can enable information and money to be exchanged more quickly, safely and cheaply.

Quick review

- Step Five of Outside In is about partnering up to achieve a level of scale that you could not achieve alone.

- It demonstrates how partnerships can be much easier to form when you have a strategy based on creating Collaborative Advantage.

- Partnership typologies include:

  - David and Goliath partnerships, through which the innovation of small organisations can reach the market opportunities of big business.

  - New and old partnerships, through which the new ways of working created by start-ups can be combined with the prestige and authority of the old guard.

  - Strange bedfellows, through which businesses that serve very different markets can help each other to create game-changing benefits.

  - Marriages of convenience, through which businesses that might otherwise compete or not seek to support each other can nevertheless work together to access opportunities that neither party could address alone.

Step Five: strategic audit

1 Which organisations from other industries could you learn from? And how might they learn from you?

2 Which other organisations reach your desired participants? Or which other organisations would like to reach the participants you have?

3 How might you work together for mutual benefit with these organisations? How can you share your learning? Or how can you usefully reach and involve your shared audiences?

4 What resources could better be provided by a partner organisation? On what basis could this benefit both you and them?

5 How can you formalise your proposition to potential partners?

6 And how can you enhance and expand your partnerships over time?

Putting Collaborative Advantage into practice

CHAPTER ELEVEN

Solving problems in business

I don't believe I've ever been presented with a significant challenge, either in running my own ventures or in supporting clients, that creating Collaborative Advantage could not play a part in addressing.

I would also suggest that the primary obstacle at any point in time to creating Collaborative Advantage to build business opportunities may commonly be that we don't point our curiosity in the right direction. Our greatest failures to create Collaborative Advantage may likely occur when we overlook the process of exploring how others might help us better address a problem or challenge in the first place and instead concentrate exclusively on trying to respond to a situation ourselves. Maybe it is because we have grown up with a particular sense that we need to do our own work and that inviting others to help us is cheating. Whatever the reason, I would argue that the outcome is that for most of us, most of the time, most of the value that could be created through building Collaborative Advantage remains left on the table.

This does not mean that a conscious decision to build Collaborative Advantage guarantees easy solutions. Ideal solutions to problems rarely exist outside of maths textbooks. But if using this book helps you to ask new and useful questions of yourself, the people around you, your customers and potential advocates, supporters and partners, then you may be surprised by the power of the answers you find.

Collaborative Advantage can be enhanced at any point of any day in any task. And the Outside In framework can be applied as a systematic approach to optimising the Collaborative Advantage that can be created by any organisation or by any programme, product, service, campaign or initiative developed by any organisation.

This chapter is designed to pull into a single resource a survey of just some of the countless varied ways in which business value can be created through the creative application of these techniques and ideas. We'll explore with organisations large and small how they are applying the power of Collaborative Advantage to:

- raise funds

- identify opportunities

- develop optimal products, services and programmes

- take products, services and programmes to market

- achieve greater efficiency

- drive organisational transformation

- develop an engaged workforce

- drive growth in revenue

- enable the business' clients and partners to also create Collaborative Advantage for themselves.

Some business books may offer a small number of case studies that are carefully chosen to represent a flawless implementation of the book's central idea. A weakness of many of these books can be that in concentrating only on the successful implementation of their ideas – ignoring any challenges, obstacles or the general messiness that characterises real-world situations – they fail to illustrate how their ideas actually pan out in practice for most organisations.

The examples here offer individual instances of Collaborative Advantage in practice; but they could all have been handled differently and need not be taken as archetypal successes. They are mostly works in progress; they reveal the actions, largely of people I have worked with from across a wide range of organisations, to apply the power of collaboration to solving their challenges. But they also often reveal the aspects of those challenges that remain to be addressed.

They are intended to provide practical examples of how Collaborative Advantage can be harnessed to achieve increased organisational success across the full cycle of business activities from raising money to re-inventing the organisation. They also reveal some of the subtleties of creating Collaborative Advantage. More open participation, for example, does not itself necessarily lead to more Collaborative Advantage. Involving the right people in the right way is far more effective than simply opening the door and hoping someone interesting will walk in.

You might like to ask yourself, as you read through the examples in this chapter, which aspects of creating Collaborative Advantage and which steps of Outside In have been used in each case and how they have been applied. You might well go further and consider what you would do in the shoes of the people leading the businesses involved. What future might you seek to create for these organisations? How would you create Collaborative Advantage to help them achieve an even greater level of success? And what can you perceive in their examples that can help you advance your own activities? The future, after all, is created in conditions of uncertainty.

This is the longest chapter in the book, and if you would rather dwell on some examples and skip over others that is fine – you will still be able to follow the overall line of thought of the book.

Beyond fools, friends and family

Raising investment for new business ventures is a particular form of collaboration that requires an active development of mutual understanding to work out for all parties. It is said that only 'fools, friends and family' invest in the earliest stages of businesses because these are the only people with whom it is possible to build a relationship of sufficient trust with no track record to confirm the potential. This explains why it is so hard to raise investment in industries in which most of the funding is required before any real value creation can begin. Pitching films to investors, for example, can be particularly challenging because the film can't be produced until investment is secured, meaning that all that is being presented to investors is an idea.

One technique that has been developed to enable producers and potential investors to develop a shared understanding of what they may be coming together to create is called 'high concept pitching' and often involves presenting a new idea in terms of ideas that are already known. For example, I have heard that the film *Speed* was once pitched as '*Die Hard* on a bus', the film *Thirteen* was pitched as '*Big* for girls' and that *Alien* was pitched as '*Jaws* in space'. As it happens, this also explains how Pimp My Cause works as a brand that could be launched with zero marketing spend and nevertheless quickly generate engagement. The idea is presented as something like MTV's *Pimp My Ride*, but for charity marketing, giving good causes access to a world of marketing support that they might otherwise be excluded from and giving marketers the sense that they can get involved in something fun that puts them at the top of their game.

The mechanisms for raising funds have diversified substantially in recent years, with conventional approaches standing in apparent contrast with new approaches such as crowd-funding and peer-to-peer lending. Social projects and charitable platforms have led the way to identifying many of these new approaches, largely because the process of taking pledges and donations can be subject to less regulation than taking investment. But with increasing recognition from financial regulators, peer-to-peer platforms are increasing their ability to offer a full range of investment and financial services. Peer-to-peer lender Zopa, for example, was given the green light by the Financial Conduct Authority in 2017 to launch a new Individual Savings Account (ISA) in the UK, which makes peer-to-peer lending available in a format that allows for investment within an official tax shelter. It is also increasingly possible to use online platforms to make advanced sales or sell shares in a new venture.

Yet as a friend of mine once put it, 'Crowds can't ever really be sourced.' While the forms of raising investment may vary, an active process of creating Collaborative Advantage remains key to success whatever approach is chosen. What are you seeking to achieve? How do all parties benefit from the successful achievement of that goal? What fail-safes can be provided to make it easier for people to join in? What role can supporters play in attracting investment? How can early investors use their own influence to reach subsequent backers? Success will depend upon engaging investors in buying into the value that together you can create, deliver and capture.

This observation is as true for global PLCs as it is for start-ups. CEOs of the world's largest companies cannot work against the desires of their shareholders for long. Which is perhaps why some CEOs are working hard to influence the kinds of investors who choose to invest in their business in the first place. Paul Polman, the CEO of Unilever, for example, has maintained ever since he took the top job at the global consumer goods giant that he only wants to attract investors who buy into the long-term vision expressed in Unilever's sustainable living plan.[*] The plan is intended to balance profit with concerns for social

* www.unilever.co.uk/sustainable-living

impact and environmental sustainability. He even took the decision to withhold quarterly earnings reports specifically to create an environment that could attract investors who prioritise long-term value creation over short-term profiteering.

Complete the sequence: Talk, write, click, tap and . . .?

Khalid Aziz is a senior marketer and an advisory board member of Pimp My Cause. Earlier in his career he was director of strategy for the mobile network EE. He lifts the lid on the extraordinary breadth and depth of collaboration that can be required to develop a new mobile proposition and bring it to market. 'While telecom operators have a long track record of working with external partners to develop shared approaches to infrastructure behind the scenes, such as through the joint development of 2G, 3G and 4G network standards, working together to develop consumer-facing innovation is relatively new. The development of mobile contactless (technically known as "NFC" or "Near Field Communication") has harnessed Collaborative Advantage to create a consumer proposition that can benefit the industry, our partners and our customers.'

EE and other mobile operators knew that 'mobile contactless' could open the door to enabling people to use their smartphones to make purchases in shops, pay for public transport, collect and redeem loyalty points, buy and store tickets and access richer digital information, such as information on exhibits at museums. 'At EE we prioritised mobile payments, starting work on them as early as 2009. Consumers had already become used to talking, writing and clicking on their phones. EE now wanted to introduce "touching" to pay for merchandise.'

It was clear from the start that substantial collaboration would be required. While market research indicated consumer interest in the potential for mobile contactless, in order for its usage to catch on, this would require widespread availability of enabled handsets and payment points and a robust solution to addressing security concerns. 'None of this could be provided by EE alone, so we instigated a movement to develop a complete mobile contactless eco-system, involving all the key players who would have to work together and rely on each other to successfully stimulate consumer adoption.'

The eco-system would only work if everyone benefited. EE was a pioneer in Europe for promoting the development of mobile contactless services and drove the development of a vision for Collaborative Advantage, setting a shared industry agenda of co-creating a 'subscriber identity module (SIM)-based, fully interoperable solution that reduces industry fragmentation and creates a market with increased competition and greater consumer choice'.

To create an environment conducive to external participation, EE's executive leadership team made mobile contactless a key strategic priority and set four clear objectives:

- Deliver the first commercial launch with Barclaycard in the UK as launch partner.

- Seed the market with contactless SIMs and handsets.

- Focus on eco-system development.

- Promote pan-European operator interoperability.

As Khalid explains, 'Five sub-work streams were to be delivered by March 2011 with each operator responsible for an "element of the pie". For example, EE was responsible for the interface, Vodafone responsible for handset requirements and so on.'

After substantial trialling, EE launched the first mobile payments service in May 2011. 'For the early adopters – who tended to be more digital savvy – the key positioning was centred around starting a new movement.' The benefits offered were:

- **Convenience**: fewer cards to carry in your wallet or handbag.

- **Speed and simplicity**: tap your phone on the reader and go.

- **Security**: SIM card-based security, which is more secure than contactless payment cards. The maximum chargeable amount was initially limited to fifteen pounds.

To make the launch proposition more compelling, a strategic launch partnership was formed to support adoption and repeated usage of mobile contactless. EE developed a strategic partnership with Samsung alongside Barclaycard. And EE leveraged the Barclaycard co-branding to further address consumer security concerns. Consumer testing showed that the Barclaycard brand contributed solidity, security and financial know-how while the Orange brand – still being used by EE at that point – was perceived as younger, more innovative, customer-centric and more closely aligned to personal lifestyles.

The service was offered to customers who had a Barclaycard credit card or Barclays debit card and a particular mobile device chosen to pioneer the scheme. The service was branded 'Quick tap' to highlight the proposition based on speed and simplicity. And, over time, a greater range of handsets were introduced, that were more strongly suited to engaging the early adopters whose influence was so crucial to spreading the adoption of mobile payments across society. A strategic promotional launch offer was developed to further drive incremental sales. Customers who activated the service were given ten pounds to spend using mobile contactless and received ten per cent cashback on all mobile contactless purchases for the first three months.

It was also very important to have a wide range of retail partners where the service would be available due to the technical infrastructure upgrade cost and time required. A business development team identified and approached a list of launch partners. McDonald's, Eat, Boots and Pret A Manger were the first retailers signed up.

It was necessary to identify a powerful win–win opportunity to successfully build Collaborative Advantage. For retailers, the key benefit was reducing customer queuing time, which led to significant cost savings and incremental sales. At launch, there were fifty thousand stores with contactless readers in the UK and some 12.9 million Barclaycard credit and Barclays debit cards in circulation.

'To drive scale, EE developed an epic goal to engage its external partners. EE wanted to make the 2012 Olympics in London a mobile contactless competition, with transactions, transport and tickets all available via contactless technology.'

Khalid concludes by explaining that, while over ten per cent of financial transactions in the UK are now completed on smartphones using mobile contactless technology, fostering adoption is taking time and investment. 'During this time, an alternative innovation may even leverage the eco-system and become more successful. This has become evident with the growth of contactless credit and debit cards. Some people still believe the future is mobile payments and the hockey stick effect is just around the corner. But which propositions will gain most traction? Those of the mobile operators, the banks or technology players like Apple and Google? Or even those of cryptocurrencies such as Bitcoin? Whichever businesses create the most value will have to do so through Collaborative Advantage, unlocking significant partnerships and driving large-scale participation. Watch this space . . .'

On a mission to sell

Paul Stacey had a life ahead of him as a professional footballer and was trialling for Manchester United's academy. Then a lower-back injury struck and ended his career before it had begun. Having believed from a young age he'd be well-placed to follow his dreams, Paul couldn't face the prospect of seeking an ordinary job when leaving university. So instead he rolled the dice and launched his own business with a couple of friends from his course in software engineering.

Motivated by the goal of becoming his own boss and using the business to live life his own way according to his own priorities, he first experimented with launching an online dating site called 5minute-flirts, which used video to give people five five-minute speed dates over the internet. Then he started a business in ticket sales, launching Fatsoma, which he explains 'was a combination of the word "Fat", which was the name of the bar my co-founders and I met in and "Soma", a fictional drug from Aldous Huxley's *Brave New World* that represents the need to escape the rat race and live life on your own terms'.

This time Paul was able to embed his own philosophy in the core proposition of the business. He didn't want to be the next Ticketmaster. He wanted to do something more unique and invite others to share in his empowered approach to designing his own life. He wanted to convert selling tickets into the opportunity to lead an independent life and to support others in enjoying their lives with their friends and families. The brand agenda he put at the heart of the business is to 'Do more of what you love with the people that matter'.

This proposition elevates the core activity of the business from buying and selling tickets to enabling people to live their own lives in their own way. The Fatsoma app helps people discover events and experiences that interest them, plan those events with their friends – including where they might meet up and drink, eat or relax – and to make the most of their time. It also makes offers built around their own choices rather than foisting something on them from whichever company happens to be running the event they are attending.

The mission has also shaped the core business model that Paul has developed, creating opportunities for organisers to sell out their events, for media partners to help their audiences find experiences that match their interests and for re-sellers to be their own bosses.

As Paul explains, 'Everything we do is designed around creating value by supporting all our key stakeholders in pursuing our core brand agenda in different ways. For re-sellers the proposition is to work for yourself with an independent role that fits in with your lifestyle and allows you to build relationships with local businesses, offer and support the Fatsoma product and earn money in the process.' They can then progress onto additional activities as they become more involved in the business, with opportunities to build their own audience and promote experiences to the audiences they cultivate, leading to additional commissions.

'Doing more of what you love with the people that matter' is an interest shared by all of Fatsoma's key stakeholders – the ultimate customers of the experiences as well as the organisers, media partners and re-sellers.

Paul has grown Fatsoma to a team of over thirty staff and successfully received several rounds of external investment, including over a hundred thousand pounds in his first week of crowd-funding. And he has achieved market-leading positions in the UK in the youth and student markets with greater expansion planned into young professionals. Paul is now looking to consolidate Fatsoma's position in Britain and to expand internationally. But interestingly, Paul views success as much in terms of the mission as in the numbers: 'Ultimate success is about making our product truly represent limitless possibilities, providing the practical support people need to create amazing experiences for themselves and the people close to them.'

I love listening to Paul talk. His enthusiasm is infectious and I hope he feels proud of his achievements and the mind-set he brings to his work. He is one of a kind. The trouble with being one of a kind, though, is that you can't be everywhere, make every decision or inhabit every customer touch-point. He needs to find ways to increase the reach of his own influence by multiplying himself even more effectively through his workforce and through his partners, clients and customers. They all need to be able to 'own' the mission as well as he does and use it to ask themselves the right questions when addressing every opportunity.

This can help Fatsoma to scale its growth. The team can use their mission to achieve this by more systematically applying the tools of Outside In across the diverse stakeholders they involve in their proposition. This could involve further harnessing Fatsoma's differentiated mission as a driver of revenue growth, of customer, organiser, re-seller and partner acquisition and loyalty and of brand value. Every time a ticket is purchased through Fatsoma, there should be a chance to engage more deeply in living your life the way you want, with the people you most want to share it with. Ultimately, Paul would like all his stakeholders, including each and every user, to share his mission, fully make it their own and share it across their social groups.

That's life

So-called 'lifestyle' businesses used to suffer from a bad rap. In fact, to this day, when an entrepreneur is accused on a show like the BBC's *Dragons' Den* of running a lifestyle business, the implication is that they may not be keen on hard work and that they don't have a business capable of achieving a scale of growth that merits external investment. But is this rapidly changing? I'd argue that a business such as Fatsoma redefines what a lifestyle business can be, not just for the owners but for all involved. It's not about taking it easy. It's about bringing your whole self to work.

· ·

What future might you seek to create for the businesses introduced in this chapter? How would you use Collaborative Advantage to help them achieve an even greater level of success?

· ·

If you really want to be ambitious about enhancing lifestyles as a business leader, why not consider, at least as a thought exercise, what it would take to re-invent working for your business, to make it so attractive that people would pay a membership fee for the privilege of joining you? Skoll Award-winning Blue Ventures, a charity and social enterprise supported by Pimp My Cause, has achieved just that with their collaborative business model.

Blue Ventures was founded by Alasdair Harris, whose lifelong fascination with the sea and marine life led him to pioneer new approaches to marine conservation that go beyond research to involve local communities in building their livelihoods through integrated solutions to sustainability. The programmes allow for the temporary closure or permanent protection of nursery fishing areas with the reward of the larger and more sustainable supplies that follow. His approach is all about building lifestyles in the most sustainable sense: community-based livelihoods that future-proof otherwise potentially at-risk populations.

Blue Ventures leverages the fees and skills of volunteers who pay for the opportunity to participate in marine conservation expeditions in locations such as Madagascar, Belize and Timor-Leste. Expeditions include such opportunities as participating in dives to conduct coral reef monitoring and research that can drive Blue Ventures' transformative work. They also offer specialist opportunities catering for specific groups such as medical students who can undertake one of their official 'electives' that give them a chance to take part in and learn about expedition medicine, provide healthcare in a remote setting and learn about the social, environmental and economic context in which marine conservation activities can operate. Among other opportunities for further creating Collaborative Advantage, Blue Ventures is now exploring how to build closer relationships over time with their former volunteers, who have undertaken potentially life-changing work and who go on to undertake influential roles in key positions of economic life.

It's not just small social enterprises that understand the economic value of attractive work propositions. Businesses of all sizes are now waking up to the advantage that can come from deeply motivated, highly energised and more truly connected teams. Even global corporates are realising that community, health, self-development and shared purpose are crucial ingredients for a productive and loyal workforce.

Unilever has won awards for its 'Time to change' agenda that has seen boosting employee wellbeing feature as a priority of its flagship sustainable living plan. In Britain this has involved employee wellbeing 'MOTs' to measure mood, anxiety and sleep and which are accompanied with a wellbeing guide and an online hub, called 'Wellbeing and U'. Unilever has defined wellbeing as a sustainable state of feeling good and functioning well as a whole human being, physically, mentally and emotionally. The company has calculated a return on investment in Lamplighter, its global employee wellbeing programme, as a four to one ratio: a four-pound return for every one pound invested.

Aimia, the world-leading loyalty management company behind the Nectar loyalty reward card and partner to Pimp My Cause in our Loyalty for Good Challenge, has trialled approaches to enabling self-measurement of daily wellbeing and performance. The aim is to support staff in better understanding what patterns of activity maximise their happiness and their productivity. This involves taking a similar approach to innovation that Aimia adopts when developing client propositions and applies those capabilities to improving the lives of their employees.

One of the most important skills in life can be managing our own energy levels. Some types of business positively energise us while others take our energy away. The kinds of business that offer us a shared purpose that we truly buy into, that channel our creativity and that get our knees bouncing under the desk as we work, are the kinds that stand the best chance of retaining and unleashing our talent. This can also maximise the contribution we can make to the bottom line.

Spin the wheel

One of my favourite authors, the French fiction writer and diarist André Gide, coined the phrase *mise en abîme*[*] to describe the literary technique of putting a story within a story or a play within a play.

---

* Literally this means something like 'placed at one remove'. The term was borrowed from blazonry and was inspired by the idea of finding an heraldic shield divided into four quarters, with an image of the same shield replicated at one remove, for example in the top right corner. Gide mused on the possibility of finding the same image of the shield replicated again at a smaller scale in the top right of that shield, and so on, so that you could see the same image replicated again and again at further degrees of removal. If you looked through the series of shields you would ultimately see, or rather imagine seeing, the platonic idea of a shield or the 'ultimate' shield. The ultimate shield would be 'pure' in the sense that unable to be seen directly, it could also not be tainted by the false interpretation of the viewer. And yet, of course, this ultimate shield is also impossible to create. Gide was fascinated by how stories within stories can be used to construct a work of art, explore the role of the creator and shape the experience and interpretation of the reader or viewer. And we see art through the lens of the stories we tell ourselves about who we are and what we are viewing. With thanks to Professor Richard Parish, St Catherine's College, Oxford, for teaching me to 'read' French, books and life and for reviewing this tutorial note some considerable time after it was made.

Once you've used Outside In to re-structure your organisation, programme, initiative or campaign as a platform to enable the creation of Collaborative Advantage, the process can be repeated to scale the platform, building momentum, celebrating early participants, acquiring new participants and developing new propositions or partnerships. The promotion can be used to provide a 'reading' of your core business just as a story within a story may be used to provide a commentary on the story within which it appears.

At Pimp My Cause we worked with Liz Wilson, our ambassador for engagement and activation and at the time CEO of an agency called Stack to explore how we could get more marketers supporting more causes through our matching platform. Her team, including the creative director Iain Hunter, pulled together a campaign called the Year of Great Marketing Karma, a new take on our agenda of Marketing a Better World. It was launched with an app called the Karma Audit that invited marketers to grant access to their LinkedIn profiles to the god of karma and then watch as the powerful god spun the 'wheel of fortune'. Against a background of thunder and lightning the terrifying deity would assess the ethical impact of their career so far by analysing the data in their profile, before informing them of their prospects for reincarnation. The god of karma naturally gave them the opportunity to join Pimp My Cause to improve their next incarnation and also provided them with the opportunity to share their prediction on social media with colourful images of their destiny linked with invitations to other marketers to test their own fates. The app offered a fun, attention-grabbing way to involve marketers in our platform. We were able to build on its results by working with marketers who loved using it the most and by finding partner organisations interested in sharing and extending the campaign.

With zero media budget the world-first campaign went viral within the marketing profession, increased sign-ups by over four hundred per cent, supported 740 good causes, delivered a value exceeding one and a half million pounds of pro bono marketing and helped us to build strategic partnerships with professional member organisations that have continued to drive social marketing ever since.

Using Outside In to drive campaigns to refresh and scale activities that are already using the framework can help build momentum, drive new participation, open the door to the iterative testing of innovation and support you in forging new partnerships. It also has the advantage of helping you to build on and refine the skills and capabilities you have developed in creating Collaborative Advantage.

Unlike conventional campaigns that rely on heavy media investment, campaigns like the Year of Great Marketing Karma may resemble a process more akin to looking after a bonfire that increases in heat over time rather than launching fireworks into the sky that immediately get attention but burn out quickly.

Key considerations when adopting this approach might include focusing on the specific contribution to the platform you'd like the campaign to make, the goals and aspirations that users might share, the resources needed to mobilise participation in the campaign and how successive campaigns might contribute to achieving your long-term vision.

Sony united

The principles of Collaborative Advantage and the techniques of Outside In can be applied to the process of deeper organisational transformation. Steve Walker, the chairman of the advisory board of Pimp My Cause, gained extensive experience in taking a collaborative approach to driving organisational change through marketing leadership roles earlier in his career. He has continued to build on and draw upon his past in his current primary role, offering consulting services in brand transformation and leadership development through his own business.

'I spent a considerable part of my career working in the mobile tele-communications industry for large, global corporations with world-renowned brands – Ericsson and Sony in particular – as well as help-ing to build the Sony Ericsson joint venture now known as Sony Mobile from the ground up at the height of the mobile phone boom in the early 2000s. Throughout these experiences, one thing that became very clear to me was that business success was entirely dependent on collaboration and cooperation.'

Steve explains that the challenge for any executive in such a business is to harness the efficiency that comes from running a global business engine while allowing a certain degree of local market flexibility. The only way he found to achieve such an outcome was to adopt a sophis-ticated model of collaboration between global and local functions whereby both understood the opportunities and constraints faced by the other and could cooperate effectively to solve problems and be first to market with world-first products.

Early in his work in mobile telecommunications, Steve saw the need for a collaborative work style that broke with traditional patterns of the divi-sion of functions. 'I faced up to this type of dilemma many times through-out my time with Sony Ericsson. For example, when I was responsible for defining the future product roadmap, a process that typically happens three to five years ahead of market launch. We introduced an entirely new mechanism for capturing market input to the line-up.

'Typically, businesses of this nature will involve local sales organisa-tions at a very late stage in the product development cycle. This is partly because products are developed so far ahead of launch that there is a desire to avoid distracting sales teams from their key mission to maximise sales of the current portfolio, but also because a specialist skill set is needed to accurately predict future market dynamics so far in advance. My view, however, was that simply avoiding dialogue with local sales colleagues risked developing new products without taking sufficient account of customer needs and market conditions. The answer was to introduce a new type of collaboration forum that was very distinct from the traditional line-up briefings we held to introduce new products to the sales teams. These new meetings involved smaller numbers of people and only those hand-selected for their ability to think ahead and conceptual-ise the future.'

. . . .

Collaborative Advantage can be used to create value for the organisation in all stages of the business cycle.

. . . .

Combining leaders from the global product organisation with key local markets in small working teams created an open discussion environment in which true future scenario planning could take place, away from the day-to-day sales operations. Combining the intimate knowledge of experts in the development of technology roadmaps with the insights opened up by people who spent every day talking to customers enabled the creation of unique propositions capable of gaining real market traction. As Steve explains, 'The key to success was clearly defining the rules of engagement for this new collabora-tive forum, maintaining confidentiality within the group whilst vari-ous scenarios were being analysed and operating with a high level of trust that every participant had a vital role to play in finding the best solution, irrespective of where they came from in the organisation. We all knew that the success of the group depended on every individ-ual's contribution.'

The skills Steve and his teams developed in creating Collaborative Advantage through their working practices stood them in good stead when confronted by one of the most powerful market disruptions of all time. 'When I eventually became the worldwide chief marketing officer, the business had recently experienced a period of significant industry turbulence with the launch of the Apple iPhone, having just four years previously enjoyed record levels of sales and profitability. Now profits were declining and customers were being drawn to other brands more readily than ours.'

After considering all the available market and consumer insight, it became clear that a radical repositioning was needed in Sony's marketing strategy, product offer and communications, as well as a reduction in marketing overheads to free up more funds for consumer campaigns. And making such a dramatic shift across a global marketing network of several hundred people would once again require new levels of collaboration.

'As previously, I decided to bring local marketing leaders into the process from the very beginning, inviting them to work alongside leaders of central strategic functions to make sure that our end-to-end marketing plan really did recognise the diversity of the markets in which we operated and had a strong sense of shared ownership at global and local level.'

Successfully launching a new global mobile device simultaneously across around a hundred markets requires many different deliverables to come together, some produced centrally and others customised for and by each market. 'As well as combining project teams from across the marketing network, we also appointed overall programme directors whose role was to orchestrate the efforts taking place throughout the world. Each member of the marketing network knew what they needed to produce and the marketing programme directors ensured that every individual action was well-coordinated and could interface seamlessly with everything that came before and after.'

This was the first time in the history of the company that these kinds of orchestration roles had been deployed at such a high level and their presence was vital to ensure that collaboration happened effectively. Also of vital importance was a sense that everybody in the marketing network, whether central or local, was working in one team towards a very clearly defined common goal. 'Rather than feeling like adversaries, which is typical in large global organisations, we all truly felt a sense of interdependence and collective responsibility.' The results spoke for themselves. At the time, the company was able to increase its market position from number eight to number three and return to profitability.

Making cooperatives more . . . cooperative?

Open cooperation

The evolution of the cooperative movement opens a window on the fascinating ways in which the nature of cooperation and the strategies most helpful in achieving it can change from one era to another.

My first involvement with the cooperative sector came at the start of 2011 at the United Nations International Year of Cooperatives, where I discovered how much larger it was than I had realised. I was taken aback by some of the statistics, such as: one in seven people on the planet is a member of a cooperative. But at the same time I had a sense that a lot of the great work of cooperatives must somehow be hidden in plain view. However large a movement may be, if it doesn't focus enough on engaging its members as active participants in the benefits it seeks to create and as advocates to the broader communities in which they live, it risks becoming inward-looking and invisible. Indeed, many of the larger cooperatives in the world now face the challenge that most of their members do not even realise that they are members.

I saw the opportunity for the movement to grow much further through greater differentiation by extending the concept of cooperation to go beyond member ownership and formal democratic decision-making to build on its characteristics as a movement of businesses based on collaboration for the common good. I argued that it could achieve this by making itself the natural home for many of the new forms of working together for the common good that have emerged in recent years, including the kinds of collaborative and open innovation, co-creation, mass participation and networked engagement that we've explored in this book.

I was asked to develop that thinking to catalyse the start of the process of developing a 'Blueprint for a Cooperative Decade' and used that opportunity to develop a model of 'open cooperation'. I used this term to articulate the traditional cooperative model of ownership accompanied by more active member engagement, participation and collaboration, explicitly serving societal good as well as member interest. Just as there is a distinction between the letter of the law and the spirit of the law, I drew a distinction between cooperation in the sense of forming and managing a cooperative and cooperation in the sense of working together for common benefit. The latter is not just about what form of ownership and governance you adopt but also about the manner in which you manage every aspect of the operation.

The Rochdale Pioneers were credited with founding the cooperative movement in the 1840s in response to chronic unemployment and unfair living conditions. I asked what they would be likely to do today, if they were alive as young adults and potentially not in education, employment or training? I imagined that one thing they'd likely be good at is forming self-organising, self-helping networks of influence and action and I sketched out a vision of some of the role that open cooperation might play in supporting the growth of the cooperative movement.

The failure to create Collaborative Advantage may often stem from a failure of curiosity.

The vision included mechanisms to reach way beyond cooperation as a model of shared ownership and harness the power of cooperation as an organisational strategy. In short it was about making cooperatives more cooperative.

Overcoming the 'Tower of Label'

At the time, the idea was first emerging to create a cooperative trademark that could be used by all cooperatives to denote the cooperative origin of their products and services, much in the same way that an 'organic' label might indicate the environmental conditions in which food has been produced. I wondered how such an approach could actually work and mean something for the diverse range of products and services provided by cooperatives around the world.

I drew a distinction between traditional labelling schemes on the one hand and a new open platform approach to labelling on the other. Traditional labels function rather like image-based brands from an analogue era of marketing. They communicate a simple message captured in a single word, phrase or image. They invite the purchaser to trust in the authority and expertise of the auditor and, in the vast majority of instances, the information exchange between producer and consumer ends in the blink of an eye. You know you want to give developing world farmers a fair deal, so you pop the ethically certified bananas in your basket and move on.

Fair Trade and organic labels have achieved remarkable success and I believe should be supported in everything they do. But there are now so many labels that simply replicating these systems may not be the best way forward. Consumers may already risk becoming confused by what I dubbed the 'Tower of Label'. What is the real difference between a conventional banana, an organic banana, a Fair Trade banana, a Rainforest Alliance-certified banana, a local banana, a non-air-freighted banana, a GM-free banana or a European Union eco-label certified banana?

Trust in authority may be at an all-time low. People respect incumbent labels such as Fair Trade, but tend to suspect new arrivals on the scene of 'greenwashing'. Aren't they just Fair Trade-light? Furthermore, most of these labels hinge on complex standards that take time to negotiate and that are often highly specific and prescriptive. Developing the supply base takes many years. How on earth could a standard be developed that could be applied to the entire range of cooperative products and even services? I asked if an approach based on open cooperation might provide a compelling alternative. Digital age trust tends to be earned more by direct access to raw information than on placing faith in experts behind closed doors. 'Sunlight might be the best disinfectant'* is the mantra of transparency and internet-based technologies can allow for innovative applications of such an approach.

Some restaurants may display a hygiene certificate on the wall, which shows that they have been officially inspected and approved. Other restaurants take a more ambitious approach, placing the kitchen in full view of the eating area, so that diners can see for themselves how their food is prepared. An approach based on the concept of open cooperation could take the philosophy of the latter example and apply it to the development of a cooperative label.

Instead of being a simple, 'dumb' label, a mark could be created which indicates not that an expert has validated the product behind closed doors, but rather that the total social and environmental back story of the product is available to anyone who wants

---

* The comment was originally made in 1913 by US Supreme Court Justice Louis Brandeis.

to know. Not everyone will want to know, but some will and people tend to trust those members of their peers who check up on these things rather more than they trust what they are told by big business, government or even large charities (though the latter group fare better than the previous two). The label could be directly associated with a downloadable smartphone app that would enable you to scan the barcode and automatically gain access to the raw information.

The rainbow logo of the global umbrella group that supports cooperatives, the International Cooperative Alliance, is quite an interesting graphic in that it represents diversity (each colour) in unity (the whole rainbow), which is a remarkably modern message, speaking of diverse approaches to the common good and which structurally offers a perfect fit with platform approaches that are about setting a single shared stage for diverse actors to make their contribution. It has seven different colours, which could be re-interpreted as standing for each of the seven cooperative principles. The rainbow could be featured in the visual identity of the label itself and then be picked up in the smartphone app as a dynamic infographic serving to provide information about how the cooperative behind the certified product embodies each of the seven principles in its work. This could also provide a good way to build a far richer public understanding of the many various social and environmental benefits that accrue to the cooperative model as well as having the effect of inspiring cooperatives to use their cooperative difference as a more effective marketing tool.

The app would benefit from additional functionality as well. For example, it could integrate a GPS service enabling the user to identify and find the nearest shops selling cooperative labelled food or indeed be extended to enable users to identify and get involved with cooperative initiatives and enterprises in their area.

The system could be sufficiently flexible to be applied to cooperative services as well as products and could thereby achieve transformational impact across a broad spectrum of cooperative enterprises. And the app could also be hosted on a website using the .coop domain, thereby bringing more activity and familiarity to the .coop family.

Loyal to the cause

I further argued that the cooperative app could have an associated member loyalty scheme. With a member's login, additional functionality would become available, including tracking purchases and accumulating points. In an interesting twist, it might be possible to earn loyalty points through active participation in socially and environmentally oriented small cooperative projects that the movement wishes to support or to double existing points where they are 'spent' as donations to these groups.

This brings to mind a trend that I once called the 'new CSR' – Consumer (or Citizen) Social Responsibility. Traditional corporate social responsibility programmes tend to reinforce feelings of positive association after a purchase. It's that little bit extra that makes you feel you made the right decision. Reading the Costa Foundation leaflet while you sit drinking your cappuccino. A bit of inspiration to complement the caffeine. They are also rather like signing up for a charitable donation by standing order after being stopped in the street. You may feel happy to give some money – but you can't help wondering if that should really be all there is to it? In an ever more connected age, don't people often prefer the opportunity to take a more active role in their philanthropy? Forward-leaning organisations are experimenting with developing platforms to support the new CSR, integrating opportunities for their customers to contribute time and talent in a self-directed way to the cause of their choosing.

The RockCorps and Vodafone World of Difference programmes take just this approach. RockCorps partners with major corporates to offer their customers 'money can't buy' tickets to exclusive rock concerts when they contribute four hours of their time, wherever and whenever, to the community cause of their choice. Through the World of Difference Programme, Vodafone has offered their customers opportunities to 'donate themselves to charity', sponsoring customers willing to sign up for spending two months working for the charity of their choice. Vodafone World of Difference payments helped one of our marketing volunteers at Pimp My Cause pay the mortgage while working full-time unpaid for one of our causes.

Adopting such an approach through a cooperative loyalty scheme could provide a substantial contribution towards the strategic imperative of the movement to make its difference more easily understood by the public and to function as a coherent and cohesive system that is more than the sum of its parts. It would also be doing more to leverage the tremendous potential asset of its broad member base.

Check you out

One cooperative that is putting these principles into practice is the Bees Coop supermarket in Brussels, one of a new crop of cooperative supermarkets whose members truly do roll up their sleeves. Part of their responsibility of membership is to spend three hours a month working on the tills, unpacking the lorries or processing invoices. In return they are able to collectively choose which products to stock and are able to benefit from the lower prices made possible by the fact that the business is literally run by its members. The Bees Coop offers a distinctive alternative. It provides a diverse environment that people of different backgrounds enjoy coming to in common endeavour. And it makes a further social and environmental contribution through the supply of organic, fairly traded, local produce, delivered in bulk to reduce packaging.

The key challenge facing this kind of supermarket is how to scale. What mechanisms can they develop to enable their members to reach their friends, colleagues and families with the model? How might the threshold to participation be lowered? One example might be offering trial memberships, making the supermarket available for a single shop to anyone willing to spend half an hour doing something useful.

The building society that helps you build society

As mutual organisations, building societies can also draw on a rich heritage of cooperation for member benefit. Nationwide, the largest building society in the world, seeks to project its mission of cooperation for the common good with its cleverly framed corporate purpose: 'Building society, nationwide'. At the time of writing, I've been asked to design a learning and development programme to support Nationwide in making the most of this proposition. It is highly differentiated from other statements of corporate purpose in the financial services sector and can be used to unlock tremendous value for Nationwide, its members and society. But its fullest potential will only be realised if Nationwide succeeds in fully bringing it to life through all its activities.

'Building society, nationwide' functions as a great brand agenda, fully aligned with the concept of creating Collaborative Advantage. It goes beyond many traditional statements of corporate purpose in that it can be used not only to mobilise employees, but also members and other stakeholders around a shared pursuit. It reflects the mutual status of Nationwide by aligning interests around a worthwhile activity that is intrinsically valuable.

But the most transformational value of common purpose can only be unlocked through the active participation of stakeholders, including members, their friends and families and broader societal influencers such as the media and policy makers: people that we can influence but not control. This means that Nationwide's marketers have a key role to play in articulating this purpose and involving people inside and outside the business in bringing it to life effectively through the right value propositions, well-delivered and well-showcased.

If Nationwide can fully unlock the potential that an invitation to build society nationwide represents, then it will succeed in being recognised as something more than simply a mortgage and savings institution. It will occupy a new place not only in the wallets, but also in the hearts, minds and lives of its members.

Creating a climate for change

The macro-economic changes driving the power of Collaborative Advantage are raising the profile of the contribution that professional influencers can make to client businesses and causes they support. An intriguing example of enhancing a client's ability to harness the power of Collaborative Advantage can be seen in the Negotiation Support programme of the Climate and Development Knowledge Network (CDKN) platform, a collaboration to drive climate compatible development led by global consulting firm PwC. The Negotiations Support programme is the first of its kind and seeks to amplify the voices of the poorest and most climate-vulnerable countries.

For many years, developing countries, who are most vulnerable to the impacts of climate change but least responsible for the problem, were conspicuously absent from climate change negotiations. As Kiran Sura, head of the programme explains, 'The ambition has been to help developing countries influence, secure and see the implementation of an international climate agreement that addresses their needs and priorities.'

Kiran, her team and the negotiation experts they have brought in to support their developing country clients have certainly been kept busy. Over the last six years the programme has trained 1208 individuals, supported 517 negotiators in participating in international climate meetings, generated 2577 cases of legal, technical and climate finance advice and produced 349 formal submissions to the international process.

In December 2015, following two decades of negotiations, 195 governments came together to sign the Paris Agreement – a climate agreement ambitious enough to protect the poorest nations yet nuanced enough to bring the major polluters to the table. Critically, the agreement recognised the special needs and circumstances of Least Developed Countries (LDCs) and Small Island Developing States (SIDS) and secured several important provisions for these countries to manage the impacts of climate change and make the transition to a low-carbon future.

CDKN's Negotiation Support instigated a radical change in the way international negotiations work in a number of ways. Developing countries were able to harness the power of the media to take their message to a global audience, bring a human dimension to the issues being negotiated and forge unlikely alliances with developed countries such as the UK, Germany, the USA and others in the pursuit of mutually beneficial outcomes. This was influence systematically applied to create a lasting impact on the future of the planet.

Kiran experienced the importance of her work first-hand on a visit to the Marshall Islands. 'I had the chance to look out to sea from an island whose highest point is only one and a half metres above sea-level and hear the island's then foreign minister, the late Tony deBrum, speak about his quest to save his homeland and secure a home for its children and grandchildren – that, without urgent action, may no longer exist in twenty years. A relatively unknown figure previously, he went on to become the leading global voice on climate change for

LDCs and SIDS. He orchestrated the coming together of developed and developing country parties to get the deal done.'

Kiran explains how she was amazed by the degree of influence that could be unlocked by the negotiators and technical experts. 'Sometimes unlocking Collaborative Advantage can be about the determination to achieve a common goal. I was truly inspired by all the negotiators and technical experts I had the fortune to work with. These individuals knew that climate change meant life or death for many developing country communities and worked tirelessly to secure the deal the world needed. They functioned on no or little sleep and food and spent weeks and months away from their friends and families to fight for a fair and effective deal for us. Such a deal would ultimately translate into changing behaviours and actions around the world at a scale capable of making a greater difference than we previously even thought possible.'

Next on her list of priorities is maintaining momentum – despite President Donald Trump's mid-2017 decision to reverse America's commitment to the deal – and extending her work to unlock Collaborative Advantage between global business and developing economies. This includes finding new and innovative ways to leverage private sector skills and experience to help developing countries fight climate change. For example, one of Kiran's projects involves London's top climate and environmental lawyers providing pro bono legal advice to developing countries in the talks and more recently working closely with them to develop domestic climate legislation.

The joy of influence

I would argue that there is a unique reward that comes from using the tools of influence to address a significant challenge.

I have been told that people's happiness works a bit like a thermostat. If someone is a 'seven out of ten' happy person and they receive a pay rise, a year later they will likely have got over their temporary boost in happiness long ago and will have re-established a self-score of seven out of ten on the happiness-o-meter. Another way to measure happiness, however, is not just how you happen to feel, subjectively, in the moment, but rather to step back, evaluate your work and life as a whole and explore whether you can understand most of your activity through a frame that is truly meaningful to you. Participating in purposeful collaboration can open the doors to an increase in such work and life satisfaction.

Jermaine Ranger is a talented marketer but a few years ago was about to leave the profession. Disillusioned by the struggle to find roles that could really make use of his fullest abilities, he had started to become cynical about marketing and the role it plays. In the week he started looking for other opportunities he came across Pimp My Cause and took the opportunity to get in touch with some of the charities listed on the platform that were looking for marketing support. He began working with Advice4Renters, a small charity that helps private sector tenants access legal advice and support and has since helped more than ten charities to achieve their goals. Jermaine credits the process with re-awakening his love of the profession by helping him rediscover the joy of influence and to reconnect with the sense of agency that comes from applying his abilities in a way he can rightly feel proud of.

Kiran and Jermaine's examples take us nicely forward with our exploration of Collaborative Advantage. It is a fundamental tenet of Collaborative Advantage that it seeks to benefit both the organisation and its stakeholders. We've explored examples of how Collaborative Advantage can be used to create value for the organisation in all stages of the business cycle, from raising money to innovation and core product and service development and on to marketing activities, sales, promotions and ultimately to developing an engaged workforce and driving organisational change and transformation over time. And while this chapter has focused primarily on the benefits that come from this win–win outcome for the organisation, in the next chapter we'll focus on the broader benefits that can accrue to society when we can unite behind a common purpose and explore the role Collaborative Advantage can play in addressing specific global challenges.

Quick review

- Collaborative Advantage has the potential to contribute to addressing almost any problem in business.

- The primary obstacle to creating Collaborative Advantage may often simply be not thinking to involve others in addressing the challenge at hand. The value that could have been created is overlooked.

- Collaborative Advantage can be used to:

  - raise investment

  - identify commercial opportunities

  - improve products and services

  - find better routes to market

  - increase efficiency

  - drive organisational transformation

  - increase staff engagement

  - drive growth

- Ideal finished solutions rarely exist in business. Creating Collaborative Advantage requires ongoing creativity, effort and the development of collaborative capabilities.

- The Outside In framework can be used to channel the process throughout the cycle of innovation and to give new life to mature business propositions.

CHAPTER TWELVE
Addressing global challenges

Have you ever been taken over by an unexpected moment of almost indescribable peace?

People across different cultures, religions and societies have reported such 'peak experiences'.* They can, somehow, in an instant unify, integrate and help us to make sense of our whole lives or at least substantial aspects of them. They may bring with them insight, meaning and a deeper perception that we can progressively harvest for many years to come.

The day I really took stock of how much I could love marketing I was out jogging after taking some time out to meditate. Advancing as a small dot in the middle of a vast open space I wondered what the purpose was of my profession as a marketer. Could it matter and, if so, why? It quietly occurred to me that the abstract forces of supply and demand do not mean anything until marketing comes along to connect them through a mutually attractive proposition. And that done right, marketing should be about finding the optimal way to cultivate the world's financial, material and intellectual potential for the greatest possible good.

I have often thought back to that moment and seen it as the inception of my thoughts on the concept of Collaborative Advantage, by leading me

---

* The descriptor was first used by Abraham Maslow in *Religions, Values and Peak Experiences* (Columbus: Ohio State University Press, 1964).

to explore and question the very fundamentals of marketing and strategy in an attempt to understand and apply them to the best of my ability for the most useful outcomes I could achieve. That has certainly become a significant part of how I choose to understand my life's purpose.

. . . .

The greatest problems facing humanity may ultimately be entirely dependent for their resolution on our capacity for cooperation. Our ability to create Collaborative advantage may be our most strategic capability as a species.

. . . .

Our most important capability?

We have explored throughout this book how Collaborative Advantage can be used to remove the upper limits on what an individual business or single organisation can accomplish by bringing more of the outside world in. This can de-couple the potential for growth from the level of resource owned, managed and controlled. But just how much of a contribution can be made by building Collaborative Advantage? What benefits can be created across society by this way of working?

Looking at such diverse challenges as poverty, climate change, political violence and mass migration, I have become increasingly fascinated by the observation that the greatest problems facing humanity may ultimately depend above all on our capacity for cooperation. This has the potential to further make our capability to create Collaborative advantage the most strategic asset we may have as a species.[*]

* See for example Yuval Noah Harari's *Sapiens* (Vintage, 2015) and *Homo Deus* (Harvill Secker, 2016) for his analysis of *Homo sapiens'* unique ability to create narratives that drive large-scale cooperation as the key driver of our unique evolutionary success so far.

Politicians love to talk about the need for competitiveness. And yet, in so doing, they perhaps overlook the degree to which our wealth is a product of our ability to work together. Today I'm writing in London, a capital city that owes so much of its rich cultural and economic history to the fact that it is connected by the river Thames to a world of international discovery, exchange and commerce. Doesn't our greatest wealth stem from the opportunities we have to connect?

One of the most important things we can do for the world is to generate economic value for ourselves and for others. When we pursue the creation of Collaborative Advantage to build our businesses, we are, I believe, already on to a very good thing. But this chapter is dedicated to the role that Collaborative Advantage can play in directly addressing particular global challenges.

During the years that I have worked on developing and applying the concept of Collaborative Advantage, the agenda of social and environmental issues has evolved considerably. Understandably, for example, in the wake of the financial crisis of 2008 and the subsequent international economic downturn, much of our attention shifted from longer-term environmental considerations to thoughts about what, for many, were more immediate concerns of social welfare.

At the time of writing, a key topic of enquiry is how to address increasing political instability. This is manifest in different but often connected ways, in the form of the collapse of governance in the most unstable parts of the world and in the withdrawal of support from substantial tranches of the domestic population for the incumbent parties of representative democracy and the institutions of international cooperation and collective governance in many developed parts of the world. How can we best negotiate the increasingly surprising times in which we live? How can we protect ourselves from the potential consequences of negative surprises? And how can we increase our collective exposure to the opportunities afforded by positive surprises?

Collaborative Advantage as a concept does not prescribe answers to these questions and nor is it intended by me to contain within it any particular social or political bias, beyond the observation that, by and large, creating more benefits for ourselves and for others is intrinsically a useful and interesting thing to do. Creating Collaborative Advantage does not guarantee a positive outcome. But if you want to achieve something worthwhile, creating Collaborative Advantage is likely the most effective way to go about it. Collaborative Advantage offers a practical approach and a set of tools that can be used by its practitioners to build fruitful responses to these challenges that can harness our collective capabilities and aspirations.

When we look at issues that concern us through the lens of the analysis in this book, we can perceive both their causes of and also the potential solutions to those problems differently: as failures or successes in building Collaborative Advantage. This can give us a renewed sense of agency, optimism and even responsibility. It challenges us to be more ambitious in actively fostering the changes we seek to bring about and provides us with the tools to set about the task.

While the particular priorities and interests of each reader will vary, the rest of the chapter presents an extended exploration of the role that Collaborative Advantage might play in addressing a challenge in which I have taken a particular interest: the demands of humanitarian crises and disasters. My hope is that the text lends itself to being read creatively and that you will be able to use this particular illustration as a launching-off point to inspire your own thoughts and actions in addressing whichever challenges most interest you.

UN 2.0

The Swedish philanthropist László Szombatfalvy founded the Global Challenges Foundation to provoke deeper understanding of the most pressing global risks to humanity and to catalyse new ways of tackling them. The institute offered a five million dollar prize for the best ideas for remodelling global cooperation or as they frame the challenge, 'Creating United Nations 2.0'. In Szombatfalvy's own words, 'Our current international system – including but not limited to the United Nations – was set up in another era, following the Second World War. It is no longer fit for purpose to deal with twenty-first-century risks that can affect people anywhere in the world."*

While the contribution that can be unlocked through collective cooperation may be great, the frameworks and institutions for collaboration that exist at the level of global governance may not be fully equipped to unlock the kinds of engagement, participation and collaboration that are most urgently required.

Each of us increasingly has the capacity to affect others around the world as well as at home. And each of us is affected by the actions of others around the world, even in our most domestic interests. The most important solutions must therefore involve and incentivise all of us as well as the businesses we work for, the voluntary sectors we support, the governments we elect and the education systems that our future leaders learn from. Nothing less than whole-of-society solutions can best address our most pressing issues.

A world of risks

Although the conflict in Syria has done much to change this, if we are asked to picture a 'humanitarian crisis' in our mind's eye, some

* Letter from the founder available at www.globalchallenges.org

of us may likely still imagine a drought or famine, perhaps in Africa, usually in a rural location and exacerbated by poverty. Certainly, if we are westerners, there is a good probability that we are imagining something far away, out of our reach and at what may feel to be a safe distance. Yet this picture has lost much of its relevance. The world's crises are becoming more urban, more frequent, more political, more spread out and with a greater range and complexity, as well as with knock-on effects that reach further. They can affect us all.

In 2018, according to the UN's Global Humanitarian Overview, more than 135 million people across the world may need humanitarian assistance and protection.*

But even this picture does not reveal the degree to which we may all be more vulnerable to risk than we may realise. I have been involved in shaping new ways to understand the risks of the present and of the future through a piece of work with Dr Randolph Kent at the Humanitarian Futures Programme that was run for a decade at King's College London. Randolph, a visiting professor at the university, benefits from the experience of an entire career addressing the most challenging crises having been the UN resident coordinator, the most senior UN official on the ground, for some of the largest scale crises of recent decades.

Randolph analyses the future implications of changes in society, technology, security, human vulnerability and humanitarian crises and identifies the risk of entire categories of crisis for which we are universally ill-prepared, including 'simultaneous crises', 'cascading risks', 'synchronous failures' and 'existential threats'. Individual examples of risk such as the threat of 'engineered pandemics' could be more deadly and spread more quickly than anything we've ever known. Randolph is far from alone in his identification of our exposure to greater levels of risk than we generally perceive.

* www.interactive.unocha/org/publication/globalhumanitarianoverview

For example, in 2008, a collection of experts on different global catastrophic risks at the Global Catastrophic Risk Conference at the University of Oxford collectively suggested a nineteen per cent chance of an entire human extinction over the next century, albeit sensibly advising against taking the apparent precision of the finding too seriously.

A greater complexity of risk profile means greater uncertainty concerning the nature of future problems and solutions. A clear implication is that no one organisation or even sector can prepare for everything using its internal resource alone. This brings with it the need to depend on people and groups we are not in charge of, which in turn involves relying on influence rather than control.

This shift opens the door to pioneers of Collaborative Advantage to enlarge the imaginative space in which crisis response is anticipated, planned, delivered and enhanced. A further implication is that the best solutions may often begin not with systems of global governance but with the capabilities of the people affected by risk (which, the astute reader will have already concluded, is each and every one of us). As Amanda Ripley, author of *The Unthinkable* puts it, 'The more disaster survivors I met, the more I became convinced that the solutions to our problems are not necessarily complicated. They were more social than technological.'*

The existing approach to humanitarian action can arguably already not keep up with the escalating need. The humanitarian system often does not get to crises quickly enough, stay there long enough or deliver enough support to truly solve the most pressing problems. More fundamentally, it is arguably poorly geared up to understand the demands that may be placed on it by the future implications of today's risk profile.

* Amanda Ripley, *The Unthinkable* (London: Random House, 2008).

Making a humanitarian of everyone

The only way we can deliver a proportionate response may be to do substantially more to make a humanitarian of everyone. If there is a problem for the whole of society it also requires whole-of-society solutions. Today, one in 35,000 people is a humanitarian. They can't meet the needs of the remaining 34,999 people. With a world population of over 7.4 billion that means we have just over 200,000 humanitarians. They can't look after everyone in need. Even if we widen our lens to encompass civil protection and other resources available within individual states to address internal crises, the gap is not closed. The scale of the challenges can dwarf the existing solutions as well as the diversity of knowledge required to implement them.

It is no small task to better harness the world's collective talent, resources and insight to more effectively address the consequences of risk. Engaging a whole-of-society response will require accessing fresh sources of motivation, identifying new opportunities, providing different types of support, finding new ways to unlock accountability, developing new business models, achieving an unprecedented scale of collaboration and working with new types of expertise.

Conventional approaches to humanitarian response are based on a set of business models, priorities and principles that cannot be shared by everyone. There can be something 'otherising' about formalised approaches to humanitarian work. NGOs, for example, are defined by what they are not – non-governmental organisations. And if we take the 'humanitarian principles' of humanity, neutrality, impartiality and independence, at least two and arguably three of these principles are defined by what they are not – partial or partisan.

There are, of course, good reasons for formal humanitarian organisations to subscribe to these principles as a demonstration that they exist to preserve all human lives. They count on this to justify their mandate for operation. In many cases their own safety depends on the acceptance on the part of all sides in a conflict of their neutrality. And there are many parts of the world where these principles have much more to contribute to new groups seeking to extend the contribution that formal humanitarian work can make. But while we all share a common humanity, the very reason many of us across society may be motivated to address risk or the consequences of risk in the form of a disaster or emergency may be precisely because we are *not* neutral, impartial or independent but have loved ones and people whom we care about and our own preferred values to support and uphold.

This could mean a new type of activity needs to be defined that more easily makes it everyone's business to address the threats and consequences of crises. And that would involve defining a new role for the humanitarian sector in building its own Collaborative Advantage by making itself the platform to catalyse, enable and influence the participation of other sectors. This would mean creating a new paradigm for humanitarian action that is inclusive, collective, self-motivated and reaches parts of society that conventional approaches cannot.

. . . .

Surthrival goes beyond existing concepts of crisis-related action and transcends formalised approaches to humanitarian altruism. We see it as in our own interest to help ourselves and others.

. . . .

A new approach needs to be defined that we can all subscribe to because it is in all our interests. We begin building Collaborative Advantage to improve our ability to address risk by understanding the problem in terms of such a common pursuit. A brand agenda can be used to define the activity participants can involve themselves in.

I call this approach 'Surthrival' and define it as the process of growing stronger in a world of complex risks.* Surthrival goes beyond existing concepts of crisis-related action. It transcends the formalised approaches to humanitarian altruism because it is in our own interests to help ourselves and others. It goes beyond risk reduction and response because the world may face advanced persistent threats but human ingenuity can also find advanced persistent opportunities. More than building resilience to shocks, Surthrival is also about actively increasing our success in an unpredictable environment. And it reaches beyond the work of 'continuity planning', because Surthrival doesn't just allow us to continue our lives and businesses, it allows us to enhance them.

Surthrival unlocked

The pursuit of Suthrival is fertile ground for developing Collaborative Advantage as we collectively learn how to tune into it.

Surthrival involves building capabilities that are relevant to all our lives and to all our organisations to help us succeed in environments that appear increasingly complex, surprising and unpredictable. It involves the ability to build a clear purpose, capable of attracting the participation of a coalition of the willing. The Outside In framework explored earlier in this book can be an excellent tool to unlock this capability. It involves the ability to learn from strangers, as an increasing portion of what we need to know in a surprising environment will not have previously occurred to us to learn. It involves being sure to protect the assets that we cannot do without. And it involves cultivating options so that,

* Nicholas Nassim Taleb, *Antifragile: Things that Gain from Disorder* (London: Allen Lane, 2012) more broadly analyses the people, policies and institutions from all spheres of life and across many geographies and histories that have the propensity to benefit from a volatile environment.

when one option becomes limited by something unexpected, we are protected and when surprising events provide additional opportunities we have options ready to pursue them with.

It can require making sure we have access to a surplus of key resources even if we do not have exclusive ownership of them. It can mean having the ability to fail with minimal harm. And it can imply becoming used to tasting danger and learning to accommodate it.

The principle behind immunisation is that exposure to a deliberate small dose of disease can enable us to build our defences against larger accidental exposures. Perhaps the concept has merit beyond the idea of injections.

All of these capabilities have a role to play not just in enabling us to avoid failure but also to succeed in an unpredictable world. Through the Surthrival paradigm the message to the world is that we live in a risky environment and the more we can get used to that and even, where possible, turn it into a positive the better.

This can involve new roles and responsibilities for humanitarians and other groups who have a professional responsibility for crisis preparedness and response. With seven billion people at risk in ways few people can truly imagine, the more humanitarians and governments can do to help people to help themselves and each other to identify opportunities in the context of risk, the better they will be exercising their roles. Surthrival implies the need for new capabilities in humanitarian organisations – especially through the application of the tools of influence – and it also implies that new ways will need to be found to measure their success in terms of the indirect actions they instigate and enable rather than solely in terms of the direct actions they undertake themselves.

Humanitarian organisations have the opportunity to make themselves the platform for Surthrival. They need to understand better and support the actions people affected by risk can take to help themselves and each other. And they can apply the Outside In framework to identify the most useful contributions they can make, build an agenda of relevance to others, create useful opportunities for open participation, build the right environment for collaboration, work with the few to reach the many and partner up to achieve more.

What risks do you face yourself? How may you be affected by the potential secondary impacts of risks faced by other people? How will you respond when hit by surprising events? How can learning to cope with complexity benefit your life and the lives of others? And how can it benefit your organisation or your community?

Meet the Surthrivalists

An increasing number of people and organisations are already learning to work in this way, using the exposure to risk as a catalyst for creating benefits that both address and reach beyond the immediate need. Development Media International, one of the charities supported through Pimp My Cause, runs radio and TV campaigns to change behaviours and save lives in developing countries. They work with local people to create serial radio dramas that entertain local communities while engaging them in storylines that teach them how to avoid risks to which they may be exposed, such as particular infectious diseases. The output is entertaining and enriches people's lives while delivering life-saving messages that have been shown to be as cost effective as childhood immunisation.

Sometimes an individual's response to their family's exposure to risk can change the course of their lives forever. Richard Turere, a nine-year-old Kenyan boy from the Maasai community, saw the cattle – on which his family's livelihood depended – were vulnerable to attacks from lions on the unfenced south side of Nairobi National Park. He tried using kerosene lamps and scarecrows.

While these didn't work, he noticed that the lions didn't attack when people were present. He hypothesised that the moving light of torches dissuaded the lions by making them think humans were approaching. By the age of eleven he was able to replicate this effect by connecting LED lights (charged during the day with solar panels) through an old motorbike indicator box to make them flash intermittently. He protected the cattle, was soon asked to make the system for neighbouring farms and ultimately won a scholarship to Nairobi's private Brookhouse school and achieved deserved global recognition for his skills in innovation.

My friend Ken Banks invented a system of mass communication by text message for use in large-scale crises to provide the key information affected populations might need to survive. But one of his favourite deployments of the resulting FrontlineSMS technology came when a group of NGOs used it to monitor the 2007 Nigerian presidential election, an application he could in no way have foreseen when he created the platform.

Practitioners of Surthrival already exist among governments as well. The 2014 Commonwealth Games in Glasgow was the site of the biggest security operation in Scotland's history. The exposure to the potential threats that a large-scale, high-profile public event can bring with it forced the city to upgrade its security protocols, which have given the games a legacy of increased public security.

And when Cuba developed a high level of expertise in fighting pandemics and as a matter of national pride sent more doctors to west Africa to deal with the 2014 Ebola pandemic than any other country, they ultimately secured many unexpected new diplomatic allies, from US Secretary of State John Kerry to the pope. This ultimately opened the doors to the potential for new levels of prosperity for Cuba as a nation that, with this new support, started to overcome the antagonistic relationship with the USA which had restricted Cuba's economic development since diplomatic relations were severed in 1961 during the cold war. The developments contributed to the re-establishment of these relations during President Obama's second term in office.

Surthrival for change

If Surthrival provides an alternative *to* humanitarian action, perhaps the alternative *for* humanitarian action is to enable Surthrival by driving change. This can best be achieved by re-imagining the sector and the actors within it as platforms enabling people to Surthrive. Collaborative Advantage can offer a model for systematically re-imagining sectors, organisations, initiatives and campaigns as platforms for maximising success through external participation.

Early examples already exist in the humanitarian sector. We previously saw the Start Network identify the fact that crises often suffer from a humanitarian response that is absent, late or of poor quality. They address this by setting the agenda of connecting people affected by crisis with the best possible solutions. Each crisis strengthens the adaptive capacity of the network. Each activation of the Start Fund drives evolutionary improvement by selecting the best option that can be made available.

Many other territories exist to harness the potential of Collaborative Advantage to contribute to the Surthrival agenda. A suite of initial sketches can be used to illustrate just a few of the possibilities.

Surthrival insurance

One of the key reasons that populations exposed to potential disasters remain vulnerable is their lack of access to insurance. Insurance is one of the most overlooked tools to combat the after-effects of a disaster and can also be a powerful tool to mobilise effective work in disaster risk reduction. It can also assist prevention, through advisory services provided by insurers and the reduced premiums that can be achieved when risks are mitigated.

The potential exists to substantially enhance the protection of some of the world's most vulnerable populations who today remain without financial cover. Insurance companies can develop specific programmes for at-risk populations and work collectively with inter-governmental agencies to build conditions that enable the authorities responsible for more of the world's most at-risk populations to insure their key infrastructure. It's also about taking action to bring down the cost of that insurance by undertaking measures to reduce their exposure to risk or increase their ability to mitigate the effects and the costs of the disasters to which they may be most exposed.

In a digital age, could we not be more ambitious, more connected and more participatory in our approach? 'Surthrival insurance' could draw inspiration from telematic approaches to car insurance, such as those that we briefly looked at in our earlier easyCar case study. When a driver installs a telematics system in their car, the insurer automatically receives a huge amount of data about the user's driving and this can dramatically affect the calculated possibility of an accident, thereby allowing an insurance premium to be fixed that reflects the specific risk profile of the driver in practice. After all, should a twenty-one-year-old male driver who happens to be one of the most observant, considerate and safe drivers on the road be forced to pay an annual premium that reflects the fact that too many people in the same demographic may be boy-racers? Telematic insurance programmes align the interests of the insurer and the insured and, by communicating the results of the data to the user along with an explanation of their premiums, can actively educate drivers and foster greater safety on the roads. This is a win for everyone and enables insurers to offer revised premiums every three months – rather than just once a year – to allow users to make the most of the learning available.

Could a similar approach be taken to provide micro-insurance for the world's most disaster-threatened populations to support them in taking actions that protect their supply chains, public infrastructure, private businesses, farms and livelihoods? Furthermore, could we all access professional, business, personal and public insurance products that actively enable us to learn to reduce risk and then save money on our premiums and reduce the potential harmful effect of things going wrong?

The Surthrival index

Financiers can make innumerable contributions that may enhance our ability to contend with risk. A Surthrival index could be just one such approach. Arguably, the most powerful influence that engaged the world's largest corporations in taking environmental sustainability seriously was not so much campaigners demanding change (as important as they may have been), but financial analysts beginning to ask companies to measure and communicate their environmental performance data. This was regularly published in league tables. This made sustainability a CEO-level concern within the business as it could directly affect share price.

How could we measure, report on and share Surthrival performance metrics? By country, company, community, household or even individual?

The Surthrival app

As I've argued throughout this chapter, a sad truth is that we may all be exposed to the risk of crises, emergencies and disasters to a greater degree than we realise. Could Surthrival apps draw on the key trends of the Internet of Everything, big data and communities of shared purpose to identify and rank the likelihood of hazards and to enable co-created plans for addressing them?

An app already exists specifically to support organisations in North America. In Case of Crisis* can be launched by, for example, universities keen to help protect their students from the harmful effects of risks, ranging from adverse weather conditions to the outbreak of a major infectious disease. In Case of Crisis is associated with a template that can support universities in developing crisis response plans that may not even have existed before the prompt to work with the system. Students are asked to download the app to their mobile phones when they enrol. In the event of a crisis, they can then be fed information in real time to alert them to the threat and to support them in taking appropriate action.

Let's say, for example, a man with a gun is identified on campus. Students can immediately be informed of the threat and advised on the safest route to escape. The app can also be used to enable students to contribute information. For example, if a student spots the gunman changing direction, this can be fed into the system to enable new escape routes to be calculated. The app can even convert the student's phone into a flashlight in the case of a power outage.

Surthrival Aid

Could Surthrival also have implications for the way we engage large-scale activist movements for change?

Live Aid was a mass concert in 1985 to encourage charitable contributions to the Ethiopian famine that tragically claimed four hundred thousand lives. Live Eight, twenty years later, presented a message in

* incaseofcrisis.com

support of the Make Poverty History campaign. If Live Aid was about charity, Live Eight was about politics and recognised that the rules of the game of globalisation had major impacts on endemic risk.

Might there be a new space opened up for Surthrival that goes beyond charity and politics to recognise that actually, above all, 'It's about us'? We each have the power to contribute to a safer, more prosperous world for ourselves and others. Surthrival Aid concerts and events could help people engage with the practical opportunities available to them to protect themselves, the people they love and the people around the world whose risks they inevitably share.

United Beyond Nations

Surthrival can have a role to play in humanitarian reform and asks new questions of humanitarian practitioners:

- When serving the needs of people in conflict, how can we best empower people even in the most difficult situations to help themselves and each other?

- When developing humanitarian effectiveness, how can we measure the degree to which non-controlled resources are successfully harnessed to contribute to humanitarian goals?

- When driving transformation through innovation, what ideas and practices from beyond the humanitarian system can be co-created to drive breakthrough progress?

- When seeking to reduce vulnerability and manage risk, how can we work in a distributed way to use everyone's eyes in anticipating crises and engage right across society in prevention and preparedness?

When serving the needs of people in conflict, how can we best empower people in the most difficult situations to help themselves and each other?

Surthrival also challenges the model of the United Nations, but perhaps in ways that can help it get back to its earliest intentions. As Kofi Annan, former secretary general, writes in his book, *Interventions*, his desire for the UN was to get back to putting citizens first. 'For far too long the UN had been considered the sole prerogative of states and their representatives . . . From my first days in office I reminded the heads of state that the first words of the UN Charter did not refer to them – indeed, they were written in the voice of "We the Peoples" . . . Instead of leading an organisation dedicated to the governments of the world, I would put the individual at the centre of everything we did." But what if, instead of just trying to put ordinary people first, we try to support these people and the organisations they work for or belong to as the active agents of their own change?

Could the answer to László Szombatfalvy's question of UN reform be addressed by re-imagining the organisation as 'United Beyond Nations' and providing it with the transformed mission of enabling emerging forms of global collaboration? Could its convening power be better leveraged by actively bringing together more than the usual players to meet, share views, collaborate and strengthen the contributions that much broader swathes of society can make? How might its impacts be increased by enabling much broader groups to access opportunities, reduce duplication of efforts, accelerate the adoption of ideas, build standards and identify from the best of all disciplines what works in addressing global problems?

* Kofi Annan, *Interventions: A Life in War and Peace* (New York: Penguin, 2012).

The Leading Edge

I've been fortunate enough to apply this approach in seed form through a programme developed by the UN's Office for the Coordination of Humanitarian Affairs with the support of the British and Swiss governments.

To advance the frontiers of crisis preparedness and response they launched the Leading Edge Programme, a collaborative problem-solving platform that supports networks of practitioners in crisis preparedness and response and other interested groups in collectively identifying, selecting and solving pressing humanitarian challenges. These actions are framed with clear objectives, leading to tangible outcomes in definable stages of achievement that collectively add up to making improvements in particular components of how crises are addressed on the ground. The programme seeks to amplify work already taking place in civil protection and the humanitarian system, open up new collaboration across functions and more actively welcome meaningful contributions of participants from outside these networks. It is also intended to recognise and support activities that spin out of the programme, bringing these diverse groups together. It builds Collaborative Advantage by mobilising participation, unlocking new sources of solutions, supporting the pioneers and champions of those solutions and making the outcomes visible and shareable among practitioners to foster a broader process of dynamic change.

The 'Edge' of 'Leading Edge' refers to the 'edge' of the frontline of response as well as gaining a professional 'edge' in how the frontline of response can be provided. And the 'frontiers' of its brand agenda, 'Advancing the frontiers of crisis preparedness and response', refers to the frontiers between members of organisational networks, between networks and between professional practitioners and other groups, and above all to the 'frontiers' between what is and what might be – between how crisis preparedness and response is delivered now and how it could be improved upon in the future.

The Leading Edge Programme is already enabling an inclusive approach to identifying and solving a rolling platform of the most pressing challenges facing advanced technical approaches to crisis preparedness and response at any point in time.

Towards 2030

It is my belief that similar approaches can be taken to address the broader range of global problems faced in international governance.

....

Even the thorniest problems of political violence can perhaps best be understood as a challenge to build Collaborative Advantage for the pursuit of peace.

....

The UN's sustainable development goals, officially known as the 2030 Agenda for Sustainable Development, is a set of seventeen aspirational goals, ranging from no poverty to sustainable cities and communities, with 169 targets among them that all focus on problems that can only be truly solved by the people of the world acting together across all sectors of society. It is incredibly important to have identified these goals and the fact they have been agreed globally gives them a legitimacy that makes them one of our best hopes for a prosperous, resilient and sustainable future.

But whether the goals are achieved will likely depend on the degree of expertise, creative thinking and entrepreneurial endeavour that can be harnessed to engage the global participation of citizens, businesses and civil society. In the vast majority of cases these are people and groups who were not involved in the creation of the goals. Their behaviour and actions can, for the most part, be influenced but not controlled.

The most effective way of meeting those goals is likely to be the process of making achieving them a relevant concern to our day-to-day lives that involves us each being a part of the solution. Even the thorniest problems of political violence can perhaps best be understood as a challenge to build Collaborative Advantage for the collective pursuit of peace.

Quick review

- Creating Collaborative Advantage may be our most important capability in business and in life.

- Creating Collaborative Advantage to generate economic value may already be one of the most useful contributions we can make to society.

- Collaborative Advantage also provides a lens through which to understand how social problems may come into existence and how they may best be addressed.

- The major social problems of our time, from poverty to climate change to political violence, all depend for their resolution on cooperation among many stakeholders.

- Understanding Collaborative Advantage increases our collective agency and shows us how we can take responsibility for addressing problems that might otherwise have seemed out of our reach. It provides hope and challenges us to actively foster the kinds of changes we would like to see in the world.

Conclusion: the art of improving people's lives at a profit

I have enjoyed the privilege of dedicating the most recent years of my working life to exploring the ways the discipline of marketing and the tools of influence can be used to develop a more effective approach to organisational strategy, to help businesses to grow and at the same time to make a greater contribution to society.

As you now know, this has included creating Pimp My Cause, a social venture that helps marketers to get better at marketing by supporting charities and social enterprises with their marketing capabilities. And running the Agency of the Future, which exists to support clients and partners in putting marketing at the heart of organisational strategy to create benefits for the business, its customers and their broader communities.

....

One of the traditional defences of marketing is that it helps societies as a whole to better adapt to their changing circumstances, through the products and services that marketers launch and also through the underlying narratives or ways of perceiving the world that are embedded in them.

....

The concept of Collaborative Advantage emerged directly from this practice and enhanced it in a virtuous cycle. I have used it as the basis for helping clients to address a huge variety of challenges, from increasing revenues or entering new markets to tackling social problems such as poverty or climate change. I have also applied the approach to developing each of my own businesses. And in doing so I have found ways to better understand, better articulate and indeed improve the core concept.

A driving belief of my work has been that the set of problems marketers are usually given to solve is much smaller than the set of problems that marketing and the tools of influence can be used to solve. Never has this been more the case than in today's world where the most important challenges facing business and society are problems that no one person, organisation, sector, nation or even world region can solve by acting alone. Our dependence on cooperation for our very way of life to be maintained highlights the importance of any discipline that can help us achieve greater influence and build better relationships.

One of the traditional defences of marketing is that it helps societies as a whole to better adapt to their changing circumstances. This relates not just to the products and services that marketers launch, but also to the underlying narratives or ways of perceiving the world that are embedded in them. Indeed, ever since our minds evolved to articulate and understand imagined realities, the evolution of human culture has been driven perhaps more by the stories of imagined ideas even than by our DNA.*

---

* As Yuval Noah Harari writes in *Sapiens: A Brief History of Humankind* (op. cit.): 'From the cognitive revolution onwards, historical narratives replace biological theories as our primary means of explaining the development of *Homo sapiens*. To understand the rise of Christianity or the French Revolution, it is not enough to comprehend the interaction of genes, hormones and organisms. It is necessary to take into account the interaction of ideas, images and fantasies.'

The most fundamental insight into human cognitive functioning that I've come across so far in my research relates to the observation that we have an innate preference for functioning on autopilot. Our conscious mind is a relatively scarce resource. It can typically only be used to process seven to ten pieces of information at once and can be expensive to use in terms of calories expended. So wherever possible we do everything we can with the unconscious mind and reserve the conscious mind for solving the problems we don't yet know how to address unconsciously.

As Gerhard Roth, the neuroscientist, puts it in his article 'The Quest to Find Consciousness' in a special edition of *Scientific American Mind*, 'The brain is constantly trying to automate processes, thereby dispelling them from consciousness; in this way its work will be completed faster, more effectively and at a lower metabolic level. Consciousness, on the other hand, is slow, subject to error and "expensive".'* For example, I may know how to walk to my local tennis club without concentrating but still have to work out on the way there how on earth to deal with a particular opponent's venomous forehand.

What's interesting is that the very process the conscious mind uses to solve problems so that they can be relegated back to the unconscious mind is itself a process of *forming a narrative*. Once I've created the story in my mind of how and when to overcome the opponent's forehand, my conscious mind is then free to take on the next problem, such as working out if I have enough change for the floodlights or planning what to do with the rest of the evening after the match. This example is trivial. But the process is a deep and intimate part of what it is to have a human mind. If we can influence the stories we tell ourselves as individuals and societies, then we may have the potential to unlock a huge latent reservoir of potential to create change that can benefit ourselves and the people around us.

* Gerhard Roth, 'The Quest to Find Consciousness', *Scientific American Mind*, 2004, Vol. 14, No. 1, 32–9 www.jstor.org/stable/24939363

To give just one illustration, Pimp My Cause partnered with the agency Ogilvy to support a death awareness charity called CEDAR in developing the concept of 'Good grief'. This framing is now used to drive an approach used to support young people in starting to come to terms with the potential for loss before it happens rather than after a loved one has died.

. . . .

Through the lens of Collaborative Advantage, our marketing isn't just about telling the right story – it's about creating the right parts for our customers and other stakeholders to play in that story.

. . . .

The capacity of the concept for supporting people in reducing the loneliness and isolation that they risk being exposed to by better preparing for the loss of a loved one resides in the implicit idea that grief can be tempered by constructive action. The implication is that we are not powerless in the struggle to come to terms with grief. By perceiving it at the right time as a process that we can get better at we more easily ask our conscious and unconscious minds to find positive ways to address it. A challenge that might otherwise have presented itself as utterly intractable becomes something that we can at least prepare ourselves to contend with.

Marketing has always involved storytelling and creating narratives as lenses through which to understand the world around us and our interactions within it. And crucially, with the pursuit of Collaborative Advantage, marketing isn't just about telling the right story – it's about creating the right parts for our customers and other stakeholders to play in bringing that story to life.

Cognitive psychologists talk about how the inner narratives through which we understand ourselves and our identities – in other words, some of our most fundamental acts of cognition – are encoded, embodied, extended and enacted through the people and objects that we surround ourselves with.[*] Who we understand ourselves to be and what purpose we believe ourselves to be pursuing in our daily lives can be reinforced by everything from the books we have by our beds to the office we use at work and the clothes we wear. Our inner narratives can be further reinforced by a 'cultural ratchet' through which our shared understanding is communicated across groups and society. With and through others we develop our understanding of how to live and we form our aspirations.[†]

Through the application of the Outside In framework we have explored five steps to achieve breakthrough success by getting more people on your side and helping them to not only perceive the world or an aspect of life differently but also to take action both individually and collectively in accordance with that changed perception.

This has included framing the contribution you make in terms of what you enable the world to do better – or as I have described it, your 'brand agenda' – and orientating your whole organisation around supporting this purpose. Whether you make pharmaceuticals to help people overcome their colds, flus and headaches or provide a platform to help people make last-minute travel arrangements, if you don't help the people you serve do something better, you may not have much of a business to build in the first place. And if you can influence how people understand what they are doing and why they are doing it when they use your products or services, you will be far better placed to influence their associated choices and behaviours.

---

[*] The four 'e's: 'encoded', 'embodied', 'extended' and 'enacted' are sometimes referred to as the components of '4E cognition', a concept that is used to emphasise the extent to which thinking or at least the components of thought, are formed outside the brain in an environment that shapes and reinforces our thoughts.
[†] A excellent starting point to delve deeper into these views can be found in Vincent Deary's *How We Are* (London: Penguin, 2015).

It has also included innovation in the way we enable people to pursue that brand agenda and a process of engagement that enhances people's opportunities to pursue it alongside each other, potentially multiplying your numbers of customers in the process. And it has included methods of co-creation that help you work with your strongest supporters or most loyal and enthusiastic customers to improve your offering. We have also seen how such an approach can culminate in ways to build partnerships that can help you to scale to new heights that would be unachievable by acting alone.

My hope is that the concept of Collaborative Advantage and the Outside In framework presented in this book can help you to understand strategy in a different way and to build new levels of success around that insight. And that, similarly, you will be well placed to help your customers understand the challenges you assist them in addressing in new and interesting ways and to participate effectively in pursuing the solutions you offer them.

As a final word, I would suggest three essential ingredients that people seeking to influence others in any capacity can adopt to ensure that this influence is used ethically, sustainably and effectively. Firstly, we should approach any challenge with a desire to contribute. When we begin by addressing any question with the aim of making a net contribution to people's lives, not a deduction, isn't that just 'good business' – in both senses?

Secondly, let's always remember the value of human agency. As appealing as it may sound, our goal should rarely be to 'improve other people's lives', per se. Such a goal implies that others should be the passive and no doubt pathetically grateful recipients of our benevolence. Instead, our goal should be to enhance people's ability to improve their own lives as they wish, which is potentially a deeper and more transformative process, capable of unlocking many more relational benefits.

Thirdly, enabling change to stick and become socially engrained across markets and communities is best achieved by a systematic approach that harnesses the fullest value of every act of participation to take us closer to achieving our shared goals.

My hope is that the concept of Collaborative Advantage and the Outside In framework can serve to provide just such a framework that can support any of us in leading change for the benefit of ourselves and others in our own fields of activity.

Our interconnected world of opportunity is also full of interdependencies, risk and uncertainty. Enabling people to better grasp the reality around them and gain greater agency over their outcomes has perhaps never been a more relevant and useful pursuit.

Next time you seek to influence a friend, colleague or customer, why not stop to ask yourself how you can start by helping them to find new ways to understand the world differently and thereby choose to take action accordingly. You may be surprised by the power of the results you achieve.

Over to you.

Further collaboration

I'm always learning more about how to create Collaborative Advantage and would welcome the chance to hear your thoughts and ideas on the subject. Drop me a line at paul@theaof.com.

That's also the best way to reach me if you'd like to book me to speak at an event or engage the Agency of the Future to advise on the creation of Collaborative Advantage for your organisation.

And if you'd like to collaborate with Pimp My Cause, please contact Anna Mullenneaux at anna@pimpmycause.org.

Acknowledgements

First of all I would like to thank you for picking this book up and choosing to read it. And my gratitude will be doubled when you put the ideas into practice.

I particularly thank my mother, father, Anna and Nathan without whose support and inspiration I would not have been able to write the book or develop the ideas on which it is based.

At the Little, Brown Book Group I am deeply grateful to Nikki Read and Giles Lewis for making the book possible and for bringing their insight and experience to bear on improving it. I am also extremely grateful to Lucian Randall for copy editing the text with an extraordinary eye for detail and to Rebecca Sheppard for her support and expertise in overseeing the book's production.

Many thanks also to my clients and partners at the Agency of the Future. Working together has helped me identify, develop, test and refine the ideas of the book.

I am also grateful to the members of Pimp My Cause, who every day provide a living laboratory of Collaborative Advantage in action. Thanks especially to Steve Walker for chairing our advisory board and acting as a coach, mentor and enabler across all our activities.

I have also drawn particular benefit from my conversations and collaboration with Aladin Aladin, Heba Aly, Chris Austin, Khalid Aziz, Marina Banks, Mandy Bobrowksi, Rachel Botsman, Sophie Brown, Hugh

Burkitt, Catherine Cherry, Ben Cohen, Dave Crowther, Chris Daly, Leisha Daly, Els Demeester, Carmen Muñoz Dormoy, Valérie Abrell Duong, Diane Earles, Marion Enderlein, Alex Epstein, Mark Evans, Lynne Franks OBE, Geoff Gay, Paul George, Anne Grafe-Buckens, Gemma Greaves, Jerry Greenfield, Chuck Gould, John Grant, Juliet Hodges, Melody Hossaini, Marieke Hounjet, Dr Randolph Kent, Thomas Kolster, Christine Knudsen, Isabelle Loc, Dinah Louda, Sean Lowrie, Jesper Lund, Amanda Mackenzie, John Marsden, Simon Maxwell, Ed Mayo, Kevin McNair, Don McPhee, Jonathan Mildenhall, Klaus Niedelander, Lars Peter Nissen, Gareth Owen, Professor Richard Parish, Thomas Peter, Melissa Porter, Celia Pronto, Damian Ryan, Professor Roy Sandbach OBE, Amanda Schneider, Sir Tom Shebbeare KVCO, Anisha Singh, Sarah Speake, Laurence Stock, Jeremy Stoner, Kiran Sura, Rory Sutherland, Caroline Taylor, James Taylor, the Rev Dr Colin Thompson, Ayça Apak Tonge, Heather Wade, Adrian West, Arno Wicki, Liz Wilson, Stuart Wilson, Jackie Yeaney and Nermin Yilmaz.

Index

Wilson, Liz, 158
Women's Forum for the Economy
     and Society, 37, 81
word-of-mouth marketing, 116
WWF, 99
Wyndham's, 131

X Factor, The, 39

Year of Great Marketing Karma,
     158, 159
YouTube, 26, 61–2